To our e...

Good wishes
        and good luck

        A. Rhen

IRON PRESS

THE
ICE COLD
REVENGE
OF
JOHN DOLAN

Arthur Appleton

Autobiographical

Arthur Appleton was born in Sunderland and was working at fourteen first as a chemist shop errand boy and then as an office boy. He began writing in his teens and left his job as a clerk to try his luck in London. He was, of course, unsuccessful and as he received no dole for six weeks because he'd left a job, during the last three months of 1937 he could afford only once the price of a hot meal at a cost of a shilling. His first publication was a poem in the Observer in 1939. After service in the Royal Engineers in the Middle East, he became a scriptwriter and then programme planner with the Forces Broadcasting Service in Haifa and Jerusalem, and this led to nearly thirty years of work with the BBC in Newcastle, Manchester and Bristol as a reporter and radio producer. He has had a score of radio documentaries broadcast as well as three for television. He has covered football regularly since 1948 mainly for the BBC but also for the press and for the last few years for the Sunday Times. He has written five books on the game, including Hotbed of Soccer published in 1960 by Rupert Hart-Davis. In 1973 Michael Joseph published his *Mary Ann Cotton: Her Story and Trial* the first full acount of the infamous North East poisoner. A three half hour adaptation of the book appeared on television. He lives in Gosforth, Newcastle.

Nine of these stories have been broadcast by the BBC;
The Road in 1970 from Manchester;
The Boots, 1971, Manchester;
The Ice-cold Revenge of John Dolan, 1972, Edinburgh;
The Brave Call of Mrs Tucker, 1972, Manchester;
Edward and his wife's Infatuation, 1975, Manchester;
The Kneeling Woman, 1976, London;
The Liberation of Laura, 1977, London;
The Anniversary, 1980, London, and
A Lunchtime News Item, 1983, Edinburgh.
Mr Johnson and Mrs Salisbury was originally published in IRON Magazine, No. 48, in early 1986.

CONTENTS

First published 1987 by IRON Press
5 Marden Terrace, Cullercoats, North Shields
Tyne & Wear NE30 4PD, UK.
Tel: Tyneside (091) 2531901

Printed by Tyneside Free Press Workshop
5 Charlotte Square, Newcastle upon Tyne

Typeset by True North in 10pt Sabon

ISBN 0 906228 30 1

Front Cover design by Clare Brannen
Book Paste-up by Norman Davison

IRON Press books represented by:
Password Books Ltd
25 Horsell Rd
London
N1 1XL
Tel: 01-607-1154

THE RADIO SHORT STORY

Ten of the baker's dozen of stories here were written for radio and nine have been broadcast, all nationally, by the BBC in the fifteen-minute space usually called Morning Story. The exception is *The Commandos and the Artist*, stimulated by my reading that a reconnaissance party landed on South Georgia before that island was re-taken in 1982. The Manchester producer said she didn't think it really worked out; the Cardiff producer said it didn't appeal enough; London returned it without saying anything, and Edinburgh said it was very effective but their slot was for only one story a month and this was one of the good ones for which there wasn't room.

Now this is the usual sort of comment or lack of it which a short story writer receives, and I mention it because it shows that a radio story, like a story for a magazine, can be sent out to more than one place, in this case different BBC Network centres, and that the response is varied, and sometimes contradictory. Two of these stories, *The Kneeling Woman* and *The Liberation of Laura*, were turned down by Manchester BBC but accepted in London by Barbara Crowther, one of the most experienced Morning Story producers. *The Ice-cold Revenge of John Dolan* was also turned down by Mancheser but taken by Edinburgh, and canny Edinburgh also took *A Lunchtime News Item* after it had been sent back by London. This story was based on a newspaper report of man and woman twins being killed in Italy at the same time some two hundred miles apart, each alone in cars which crashed in mountain country.

A radio story does not need to be altered before it becomes a printed one, but one written for publication usually needs amending to make it suitable for radio. With sound being important a writer should read his story for radio out loud, record it if he has a recorder. This will make him aware among other things of awkward phrasing, distracting alliteration, lack of clarity and names being too similar. Really I should have changed the name of one of the two girls, Marilyn and Marj, in the Mrs Tucker story, probably Marilyn.

It's better to have few characters, in any case that concentrates action and thought, and most of these stories have three or four. I see there are eight in the Commandos story – more than in any other story – and wonder if this spread of interest contributed to it not being taken by the BBC. Yet the story which seems to have been liked more than any here, *The Boots* has only character fewer. Mind this story was, to me, read memorably by Geoffrey Banks, a Lancashire schoolteacher and radio actor. Rarely has the writer any effective say in who reads the story. The BBC pays the reader and the producer makes the choice. Although I once read someone else's fifteen minute story and intimated I fancied reading one of my own there was no response.

Usually advisers on radio writing say don't use long sentences, what they really mean is involved sentences. Your sentence can be quite long: the reader gives it natural breaks and it will be coherent as long as it is straightforward. Clarity is even more important than in a printed story.

In the oral tradition both first and third person storytelling can be captivating. I'm surprised myself to find that only two of the stories here are in the first person – the title story and *A Lunchtime News Item*. About first person writing Somerset Maugham thought most highly of the variety in which the storyteller character is not the main person, but is telling someone else's story. He often used this method, as did Herman Melville in *Moby Dick*. I've used this most acceptable way of first person writing in the John Dolan story.

The writer should get into the story quickly. The listener may not be prepared to give more than fifteen or thirty seconds of assessment before turning away or switching off. A reader who has bought a magazine or a collection of stories is going to be more patient.

That oft quoted remark of preferring radio drama to television drama because the pictures are better, underlines the importance of often writing in scenes – writing something which the listener can visualise. This goes for all writing. And scenes often give birth to stories. The sight of a woman kneeling close to her deaf mother to speak to her caused me to think out the story of *The Kneeling Woman*. The sight of icebergs on a trip I made to Churchill, Canada in 1956 eventually led to the writing of the John Dolan story, and *The Anniversary* is an offspring of scenes in *The Monkey's Paw* by W. W. Jacobs. But descriptions of a state of mind can be enthralling on the air too. I have had a radio story broadcast in which two thirds was taken up with a woman's envious thinking of her friend's love affair, but when action came it was explosive. The troubled thoughts of Edward in *Edward and his Wife's Infatuation* made quite acceptable listening.

Flashbacks can be used. The good advice often given, by Bernard Shaw for one, of beginning a story near its end, that is near its climax, often means that the writer has to go into flashback. Some writers say this should not take up more than a third of the length, but each story makes its own demands. It could be said that almost all the John Dolan story is a flashback, but a more typical one is that of roughly fifty per cent in *The Boots* and that proportion is right of the story.

The idea of *The Boots* came to me when my wife asked the undertaker if it would be all right placing a small silver crucifix in her mother's coffin, and in saying it would he told us that the oddest request he had had was for a pair of boots to be put in a coffin. In seizing this as a story my task was to find a reason for such a action. At the time I was writing fifteen-minute radio stories as often as I got ideas for them and this brings me to a note a short story writer's main job – the construction of his story to fit a required length. A literary magazine or a Third Programme short story has no laid down length, but for many years fifteen minutes, round about 2,300 words, has been the required length for the main radio short story market. An advantage of writing for the same market for some time is that one's mind gets into the habit of constructing for that length.

'He said,' and 'She said,' and their not so frequently used synonyms are usually necessary in print, but they can sound superflous at times when the story is read out and the reader is changing his voice for characters. Unless they can obviously be left out it is better to leave it to the producer and the reader to decide during rehearsal if some of them can be dropped.

BBC Publications have a guide: *Writing for the BBC* which includes addresses of Network Centres. These are also in *The Writers' and Artists' Yearbook*. All or most public libraries have copies of this. The book also supplies details of magazines which take short stories – possible homes for stories which you like, and feel have been imperiously sent back to you by BBC producers.

Arthur Appleton
Newcastle, June 1987

The Ice-cold Revenge
of John Dolan

The news this morning that John Dolan's preserved, frozen body has been found near to his crashed plane means, for me, that I can tell what happened on that sea trip twelve years ago.

Odd, I've thought today, if John wasn't killed on impact but lay helpless in the snow and died of exposure.

I have been thinking again of those majestic icebergs: silent, glinting, ghostly edifices, moving southward at the rate of six or seven miles a day and melting slowly in the summer sun.

I had been ill and my father got me on the trip; it was round the top of Scotland and across the North Atlantic, south of Greenland and the Davis Strait, through Hudson Strait and across Hudson Bay to the small summer-only port of Churchill in Northern Manitoba.

The ship carried a helicopter to scout out icefields. John Dolan flew and looked after this helicopter. I ate with the officers, as did Dolan. He was nearly as silent as I.

In those early days John was first to excuse himself so he could leave after meals, and at one meal, when he had left the table, the captain said perhaps it would be better if he told everyone about Mr. Dolan.

Dolan's sister, a quite beautiful girl, had been murdered three months previously on a small island off Scotland's west coast. She had gone there with a man called Masters, and there seemed to be no doubt that Masters had strangled her.

The police were still searching for Masters and Dolan had done nothing else during the three months. He was working now for more money to continue his search.

I slept badly at first, often the victim of horrific mind pictures.

When I could I geared myself to carry out the captain's advice to get a lot of fresh air and as much exercise as possible, and one day, it would be only the second or third day out, I caught a glimpse of the stowaway.

I had turned into a longish passageway and I saw a figure dart from a lavatory into a room opposite.

The next day when I came to the room – it was a storeroom – I tried the door. It opened, it was half light inside and I heard a scraping and a gasp. I closed the door and went away.

I thought of going to the captain but I knew so little of ship life that I decided I would mention it to someone else first, when I became friendly enough with someone.

The weather was often good, it was mid July, so I spent a fair bit of time on deck.

I would often watch John working from a little distance. I remember the time we first talked.

'When are you taking her up?' I said, indicating the helicopter.

'Tomorrow.'

'To check on icebergs?'

'I'll see the bergs, sure, but I'll be checking on the pack ice. The bergs are no trouble.'

'Are they not?'

'You can see them for miles. And then radar picks them out.'

Speaking with more enthusiasm than for many weeks I said: 'I'm looking forward to seeing an iceberg. Are we certain to see them?'

'I wish I could be as certain of other things.'

He flew the helicopter the next day and reported there were hundreds of bergs ahead of us.

He invited me into his cabin to see some charts and when we were sitting back having a cup of tea, I mentioned that I thought there was, or had been, someone hiding in the storeroom.

John said, 'Let's check, eh?' His eyes sparkled.

We went quietly along the passageway. He flung open the storeroom door, bent his head inside and stood still. Then he said in a loud voice: 'This is the wrong room. We don't want the storeroom,' and he closed the door.

He hastened back to his cabin.

'You're right,' he said, 'there's someone in there. Right.' He was really enjoying things. He picked up a big torch. 'I'll be on to him before he knows what's up. When I open the door you switch on every light – there are four, on the wall on the right.'

We stole back quietly and John switched on his torch. I have never seen a man move so quickly. He opened the door, sprang in, stood a moment, legs apart, listening and taking in the formation, then he darted up a narrow aisle, he seemed to run up the side of some steel shelves, leapt down, threw himself on the floor, got up and sped round to another aisle, then exclaimed, 'Ah; got yer,' and laughed.

I joined him and gazed down at the scared stowaway. A man about thirty, he was lying on layers of wrapping and sacks staring at John, his mouth open. He was bearded and dirty. He got to his feet awkwardly and then grinned.

'You should have chosen a faster ship, a shorter journey,' John said.

'I had to take what I could,' said the man. John was staring hard at him.

'Why didn't you give yourself up?'

'Why should I? And there was always the chance that he'd take me back. D'you think he will?'

'To Scotland?'

'Scotland. I didn't get on in Scotland,' the man snapped. 'I boarded her in Newcastle. What are you getting on about Scotland for? I'd had enough over there, England,' the man said. He was quite nervous now. 'Fresh start for me, I thought.'

'By the look of your clothes you were on the run before you got on the ship,' John said. He shook the man by the shoulders. 'Weren't you?'

'Well, what's that got to do with it, eh? You don't think I'd have stowed away if I'd been making my fortune, do you?' The man was pleased with this repartee and he turned to me: 'Eh? What do you think?'

John grasped the man's chin and turned his head round. 'Look at me,' he said quietly. 'You were on the run for murder.'

The man opened his mouth to protest.

'Your name is Masters, and you murdered my sister in Scotland. I've seen a photograph of you.'

The man sank back on his bed. He brought his lips together but they seemed to spring apart. He managed a whisper.

'Your sister. Your sister.'

'Prove to me you're not Masters,' John said slowly. 'Prove that to me, will you? Give me any doubt that you're not Masters, and I'll not hand you in, I'll see you fed and clothed, and I'll put you down in Canada.'

He turned to me. His eyes were hard and brilliant.

'You had better go now, I think, don't you. And not a word, of course, you know that.'

I had gone pale and cold. I had never seen men like these. I had never seen such a frightening confrontation.

The captain was not at dinner that night. He was on the bridge, using the radar and guiding us between the icebergs.

Towards the end of the meal John Dolan spoke. He asked the mate when the fog was expected to lift.

'An hour or so before light,' said the mate.

'Would you mind telling the captain I think I should go up at first light.'

The mate nodded. 'Good. You'll see pack ice, all right; beyond the bergs.'

I said to John, 'Is it possible for you take me with you?'

He shook his head. 'No. Not tomorrow morning. I leave early. I've so much to do. Some other time . . . maybe we can fix it.'

I didn't see John that evening. I went to his cabin, but it was empty. I had been sleeping better, but I got little sleep that night. There seemed to be more than the usual ship noises.

The next morning was glorious and warm. The ship was radiant in the early sunshine; the sea could not have been bluer and we were sailing between monstrous icebergs.

I was up at first light, and I dashed out and upstairs and saw the helicopter moving away to the west.

Those icebergs. I don't know of any sight which has impressed me more. I was shocked by their hugeness, intrigued by their shapes. They were great chunks of land fashioned by a giant into enormous cathedrals, animals, battleships. Their precipitous sides glinted and shone. There was one like a sea serpent, its head – hundreds of feet high – held proudly as it breasted the sea, its body and tail stretched behind for a mile or so.

The helicopter flew over them. It appeared to skim the top of the mighty wall of one of them, then I lost sight of it. When I saw it again, it seemed to be in the same area, as if leaving the berg and continuing westward.

When John returned he went straight to the captain – he had seen some icefields. He looked content when he came back on deck.

'Had breakfast?' he asked.

'No.'

'Come on, then.'

About an hour later, back on deck, I saw we were approaching the iceberg which I thought I had seen him fly over so low and disappear for a few minutes. He had his glasses trained on the berg, and I did the same.

We passed some three miles off the colossal structure and when we were due north of it I saw that the east front and wall which we had been seeing had a high lip and that behind it, and lower, there was a shining plateau.

I became fascinated by a black blob near the cliff edge of the plateau. At moments for all the world the blob seemed to become the minute figure of a man waving his arms. There was so much sunshine and glare that the figure, indeed the blob, would disappear for moments, then I would see it again.

'The bergs echo,' John said. 'Echo. The noise of the chopper going over that one . . . tremendous.'

'Can you see that blob?' I said, 'On the edge of the plateau, black. At times it looks just like a man waving and shouting to us, wanting us to rescue him.'

John looked again at the berg. 'I can see it.' His glasses stayed steady a long time. 'Probably a fissure,' he said quietly. 'The light's very decep-. tive here.'

'You'd think that was a man,' I said.

John laughed. 'If it were, he'd be finished when the sun goes down. He might as well let himself slip over the top into the sea.'

I shivered.

'Did you take the stowaway some breakfast?' I asked.

'Pardon?'

'The stowaway, have you taken him some breakfast?'

'What stowaway, son?'

'You know who I mean, John – the chap we found in the storeroom.'

'I never go in the storeroom, son. Not my territory, down there.'

'We were in together, yesterday, John. And I saw the man. You thought he was Masters.'

John stared at me and shook his head.

'We weren't in there, son. And there's no stowaway.'

I was nonplussed. 'But, John,' I said, hesitantly, pleadingly, 'you know there is, and we saw him in the storeroom, after you burst in. He was lying hidden, at the top of one of the aisles, on sacking, wrappings.'

He put an arm around my shoulders and led me away.

'You've had one of your lightheaded spells again, old man,' he said, 'mixing fancy and fact. Come on, we'll wangle another cup of tea.'

I went quiet and allowed him to take me away, while I visualised a girl left inert and dead on a green Scottish island . . . and a man alone on the glittering wastes of a slowly moving iceberg, mocked by the echoing of his crying.

The Road

He glanced up at them, trudging on. A little hot sweat dropped into his eyes and he lowered his head again, just seeing the movement of his ragged boots. The blood stains were now covered with grey dust.

'It's to be expected,' he thought, 'that they would move ahead of me.'

Noise burst near him and the young guard got off his motor cycle and stood waiting.

'Old man,' he said, 'we've got to keep moving. You knew that.' He grimaced, as if his patience was being stretched, and turned and watched the file of men ahead, disappearing round a corner one by one. Then he pulled out his revolver.

'You should have kept moving, shouldn't you,' he said.

It was then that the old man heard the sound of the aeroplane.

The author stopped there. Not bad, he thought. But for Hemingway would he have written like that? Would he even have called the old man, 'the old man'? And where was it taking place? When?

He could see the scene clearly: trees along the left – the edge of a forest; the road ahead, rising and turning away out of sight; lower soft ground to the right which lifted to rocky hillocks. Hills in the middle distance and higher hills swinging round behind them. The old man, tired out, breathing heavily, waiting; and the tall, slim young man in uniform, pleased with himself, with life.

It was just a scene. It had come out of the blue. Probably he had read it. His mind's eye took up a position as if on a hill looking down on the road and the two men. The aeroplane was visible but quiet. And then he moved in on the men, like a television camera, looking close again at the young man who was ready to kill, and at the old man who was waiting to be shot.

The old man watched the other. Just a boy, he thought, a little older than my grandson. To be killed by a youth! He heard the aeroplane again, but he hadn't the energy to look up.

'It's one of ours,' the young man grunted. 'You know your time's finished. Your kind's had it. All over, we're putting an end to you.'

The old man raised his hand a little.

'For the . . . for the time being,' he said.

He wished he had the spirit to talk so that he could, perhaps, prolong his life a few minutes; because just to stand and rest was blissful. In a second or two he would close his eyes and the young man could shoot him.

'For ever, old man', the guard said. 'It's for ever for you, anyway.'

The guard looked about. 'Wait,' he said, and he walked along the open side of the road looking at the ground.

He's finding my plot, thought the old man, my final plot.

The young man shouted: 'Come up here.' It was painful for the old man to start his body moving again. As he passed the motor cycle he noticed a short spade on the back.

'I thought the walking was going to kill me,' he said, 'then you'd have been spared this.'

The young man shrugged.

'You are younger than my son;' said the old man, 'in fact, my grandson will be nearly your age.'

'We're in a new world,' said the guard.

With his revolver he motioned the old man nearer to the edge of the road.

'I wouldn't have believed it possible,' said the old man, 'this, at one time, when I was young. I wouldn't have believed it.'

'Well, now you know.'

'I know: but I don't forgive.'

'It doesn't matter any more what you think, old man.'

Suddenly there was the noise of the plane, surging, menacing. The guard raised his revolver, but the noise was so threatening he turned. The plane was sweeping low towards them, and then there was another sound, of firing. The old man saw earth and dust shoot up in front. The young man gave an abrupt, cut-off cry, his revolver looped away, and he fell so heavily the old man knew he was dead.

The aeroplane flashed away followed by its sound. The old man gazed at the inert body a long time, for over a minute. The only movement was the slow spreading of blood. His eyes sought out the revolver, but he wasn't interested in it. Then he moved into action; going to the motor cycle he managed to open the panniers on each side of the back wheel. He found some sandwiches, two bars of chocolate, a tin of soup, two apples and a plastic flask with water in it. He left the soup, put the rest into his pockets, and hurried out of sight into the trees.

He stumbled about over high grass clumps – they were like huge dismembered heads – and they and the low branches soon exhausted him again. He kept falling and he would lie for a time, so out of breath he sounded as if he were sobbing. Then it became easier underfoot, but some small dead branches he trod on broke with a noise like a rifle shot.

He came to a path and more or less upright he moved along at speed. The path led him on to a rutted track with an occasional shaft of sunlight on it. He went along this track for a long time in a quiet, still, cool, dark green world. Then suddenly he was out in a sunny clearing. There was no one there. He slumped down beside some stacked timber, got out the flask of water but found the cap too difficult to unscrew. He lay back, was pulled into sleep, and the flask slipped from his hand.

He was wakened by the cold. The sun had gone down behind the trees. He got up, groaning at his aches, and thought he should be twenty, thirty, forty years younger. There was an open shed nearby and he shuffled across to it. He had something to eat and a drink – the cap of the flask unscrewing without much hesitation now that he had a little energy and patience.

They would have found the young guard by now. Would they send anyone after him? He doubted it. Perhaps a couple of men with dogs. That would be an end to a life: tracked and leapt upon by a dog. He thought of the guard, and of the aeroplane, but soon, warmer, he was drawn into sleep again.

The next day it was uphill work almost from the start. For a time he had to stop every twenty yards or so. Once he listened, head to one side, to the distant moaning thunder of an aeroplane. He followed a forest path for hours until clear light infiltrated and spread in front and he came out into the hills. Beneath the sun they were like mighty flowing purple sand dunes. They looked as empty of men as the forest had been.

He walked on into them and into a ravine which had a strong-running, merry-sounding stream. The ravine was fairly wide and the hills rose high at each side. Sheep scampered ahead of him. Their warning moans made the sheep at the other side of the ravine gaze across and move up the valley a little. They took up the cries until the ravine was filled with protestations, warning and lament.

Once when he saw a sheep regarding him with seeming curiosity rather than fright, he stood and gazed back at it, trying to establish some communion. Then it turned its head and walked slowly away and he allowed it to keep its unsure dignity, not moving until it was too far away to be frightened.

He pushed on and on up the valley. He became conscious only of effort and pain. His skin was tight across his cheekbones, his mouth open, his eyes glazed. At one of his stops he sank down and dozed for some minutes. When he opened his eyes he realised he was intensely miserable.

Shortly after he began his trudge again a sheep above him, oblivious of the warnings and the general movement, jerked its head and gazed at him in horror.

'Don't be frightened of me, please,' he gasped.

But the sheep hurled itself further away from him and slipped, lost all foothold and fell towards him. Miserably he watched the creature bouncing and crashing down and then come to rest near to him. There it twitched and its legs jerked then it was still. Shoulders bent he gazed at it for a longish time.

He knew now what to do. Return and rejoin his fellows. To go on was to meet a lonely death of exhaustion, exposure. Somewhere ahead he would lie huddled in coldness until death came, or he would stumble and fall and not be able to get up. If he had to die, it would be better to do so when he was with others. Maybe he could be of some small use, in some way, before that happened.

He placed a flat stone over the eye of the sheep which would be visible to birds and then he turned round and began his walk back to the road. He walked without haste, with quiet certainty and an appreciation and a melancholic enjoyment of the country about him.

The next day, when he came to the road he took no precaution but stepped out on to it straightaway. He had come out at almost the identical spot where he had left it; but the road wasn't deserted now. Less than a hundred yards away an army jeep was drawn up, and behind it and coming up to it there was a column of prisoners. There were two men in the jeep, an officer and a driver, and they looked up as he stepped out into the road. He had picked up a stick on his walk in and he leant on it and waited.

When the prisoners were nearly up to the jeep it moved forward and stopped beside the old man. The officer stared at him. He was thin, smart and the old man was sorry to see that he looked efficient and fanatical. The officer asked coldly:

'Who are you?'

'I've come from the hills, from the sheep,' said the old man. His normal voice, he realised, was disguised by weariness and hunger.

The officer continued to stare at him.

The prisoners were close to them now, and one of them, a young man, cried out when he recognised the old man. It was a cry of relief and reverence and it included the old man's name.

The officer got out of his jeep.

'So that's who you are.'

The old man nodded. So soon, so quickly, he thought.

'You were due to be dispensed with three days ago,' the officer said. 'I was told about it. It was bungled. Too much hesitation. I don't bungle.' And he pulled out his revolver and shot the old man dead.

The officer turned to the shocked prisoners.

'You, who shouted his name; get someone to help you and bury him. In that soft ground will do. Soldier, you watch them. Get a couple of spades from the truck. And see you catch us up before dark.'

The young man nearly broke down during the digging of the grave, but his friend supported him by saying that they would have found out who the old man was anyway. They laid the begrimed and blooded body in the damp ground. The young man took off his precious possession, a medallion and chain he wore, given to him by his fiancee, and fastened it round the old man's neck.

The inscription read: 'To' – it gave the young man's full name – 'whom I respect and admire as well as love.'

They filled in the grave as gently as one can do such a thing, shouldered the spades, and the soldier marched them so that they caught up the others before dark.

The author stopped writing again. He could think of nothing more to say.

Some years later, when winter was changing to spring, the author was motoring on the continent. He was travelling through lonely country, still and quiet, it was as if he were moving through a painting. The road seemed to be familiar, but he had never been in this part of the world before. The feeling that he knew the road and the land around became so powerful he stopped the car, and he realised he was in the locale of a short story he had written years ago about an old man, a captive, who had escaped from death miraculously on this road, run off through those trees into the hills, only to return here, where he had been shot immediately. The story, he remembered, had seemed unfinished.

He got out of the car and walked up and down. He thrilled when he remembered he carried a spade in the car, brought because of the snow on the high roads. He got it out and went straight to a spot and began to dig. He didn't think, he just dug until he came to bones, obviously human bones, and with them there was a medallion and chain.

'Poor old man,' he said.

He cleaned the medallion. The inscription was the same as that in his story, but he was shocked and impressed by the name of the young man. The man was now so well-known, a world figure, renowned and respected. Perhaps, the old man's return had helped form the young man, helped to make him great. Perhaps, even probably, the old man's return had been of some use after all.

The Liberation
of Laura

Laura had managed to work alongside her two daughters right through to A levels. When the younger also got to a university, Jack, her husband, admitted, nodding sagely, that she had helped.

'You did well,' he assured her, 'over all those years. Swotting up what they had to do. There must have been times, you know, there must have been times, when you didn't feel like it.'

Many times, she thought, many times when she wondered if she could be of any use to them. It had been a great and sustained challenge. She said, 'I knew, with support, they would get through.'

Jack nodded again in admiration. He had never discouraged them, he thought. And he had always kept the television sound down reasonably. 'You thought I wasn't taking notice, night after night,' he smiled, 'but I was. Take it from me, you did well, Laura.'

Laura had rarely known him to be so impressed. Experiencing a twinge of happiness, which seemed to be youthful, she realised that the opportunity for escape from the house was at hand.

The children had flown out, and Jack had genuinely acknowledged her exceptional qualities. Now was the time for the birth of that second life.

How to approach the matter?

Should she say, 'You can't expect me, with the children gone, to stay at home, just to keep it clean and have an evening meal ready for you, can you, Jack?' No, she wouldn't say that, because he would reply, 'And why not? I'm the provider here.'

If she could put it into *his* head to suggest that it would be a good thing for her to go out to work. That would be the answer. But how did she do that?

She felt it could well have to be a straightforward statement of her dissatisfaction, of her need to use her brain, to exercise her personality. But first she tried the possible loophole of a holiday in France.

'It would be expensive, Jack,' she said.

He smiled and she knew he was going to be witty.

'Would it costa more than the Costa Brava?' he said.

'Much more. . . . You know, with the children away, why don't I go back to work – I'm sure my old firm would take me back – and then we could afford such a holiday, and other things?'

'There's no need for that.' He shook his head. 'I'm not . . . decrepit. No, I'm the provider, Laura.'

'I would really like to go out to work, Jack. There's not enough to occupy me here.'

'You've forgotten what work's like, love.' He waved a dismissive hand. 'Anyway, I don't know French.'

'But I do, Jack.'

He stared at her for a few seconds. 'A man should not be dependant on that,' he said. 'And you know those types in offices: all they want is to eye young things, young tarts, dolly birds.'

'That's not so, Jack. Some of them are very busy and what they want most from a secretary is efficiency. Anyway, my legs aren't that bad.'

'No, no,' he agreed. It was true. He was a fair man. 'I doubt if they'd take you back, love. It was a long time ago.'

He got up to go into the garden.

'Jack, Jack,' she said. 'They will. . . . I've been to see them.'

He was shocked. 'You shouldn't have done that,' he said. 'You had no right.'

'I've every right, Jack. Please try to understand – we're equals in these matters. I can start any time in the next three months. They have three girls leaving.'

He was speechless for awhile. 'I'm going into the garden,' he said at last. He left slowly, then he came back, 'Oh, I'll be watching the Black and White Minstrels, and there's some football on late, at half ten. So you have BBC 2 on for yourself, or whatever you fancy, before and in-between, like.'

She said quietly, 'All right.' Shouting at him would do no good. In fact they never shouted at each other, never lost their tempers.

Laura's real pleasure was in reading. She would often manage two hours a day. Biography and modern novels: Iris Murdoch, Margaret Drabble, Kingsley Amis, and the Americans, Saul Bellow, Malamud and Updike. Also she often attended afternoon classes: to keep up with the girls, or in subjects she loved, literature, history, French.

Jack tolerated the books about the house. Occasionally he would open one. Once he said: 'What do these people know of hard work, or keeping at piece-work when you're sick to death of it, of giving up your dreams in return for a wage packet, eh? What do they know of sweat and dirt; of looking at the same machine and the same bit of wall, year after year; of bosses on your back? All this stuff, this stuff, is just sex in a nice, clean world of clever talk. They never seem to leave school. What do they know of a mean foreman, who kills your spirit? People's the trouble in life, you know. Working too hard's bad enough in all conscience, but people make it worse.'

Laura listened when he spoke like that. She was concerned. She advised him to look for a different job. 'There are nice people about,' she said. 'Why not try and work with them?' But Jack was against changing a job. 'One job's like another,' he said. She thought that was a stupid remark, unworthy of him. 'If I won the Pools, I'd pack it in,' he said.

He could not understand why Laura should want to leave the quietness, the peace of home for the turbulence of work. In the end Laura just told him outright what she was going to do.

'You've actually been back to the firm?' he said.

'They're going to pay me £60 a week.'

His eyes seemed to film over. '£16 a week,' he said.

'Sixty, Jack.'

'Sixty. Sixty. Are you sure? That's ten pounds a week more than I get.'

'It's partly because I know French well, Jack. We'll have £110 a week coming in. Think of that.'

He did not know what to say.

'I need such a job,' Laura said. 'The change. I need to do something, Jack. I must get out of the house. I've a right to a life more my own.'

He continued to stare at her.

'No matter what you say or do, I'm taking this job, or some other like it,' she said. 'You'll just have to accept it.'

'A wife of mine going out to work.' He shook his head. 'Like the youngsters.'

'You're so old fashioned, antiquated, out of touch, it's not true,' Laura said. 'I don't know why I put up with you. And in this matter,' she was flushed now, 'I'm going through with it. As I've said, no matter what you decide to do.'

He was silent a long time, then to her relief said, 'All right, Laura. All right. I'll just have to accept it. You speak as if you'd leave me to have your own way.' She was tight-lipped. 'I don't know what I'd without you. . . . Sixty pounds a week, really.'

So Laura gained her equality, won her freedom and off she went to work.

Jack was as gentle-voiced as ever, but he had been hurt. He became withdrawn, and he seemed to have lost some spirit, some defiance. She knew he had lost some pride, some self-respect. What continued to sadden him, Laura knew, was having to accept that she, after years away from work, was being paid more for doing clean and easier work, than he was being paid after working hard and well throughout the years.

She kept him in the picture, telling him of the others in the office, a lot about her boss; and of the changes, of the informality now.

The extra money was as much his as hers. He had always opened his weekly wage packet at home, taken his spending money and left the rest to her. He didn't need much. She had always wanted him to have a little more. Although he had never been well paid they had got by because he enjoyed home and garden and because she was a good manager. Now her money too went into the kitty. But Jack, took out the same amount as before. 'I don't need any more,' he said.

When she had been working for two months Jack said to her: 'Laura, why don't you stop kidding yourself? You've made your point. You've shown me, and yourself, that you can work, and earn more than me. How about packing it in, now, eh? Let's get back to how we were. Let's have our evening meal like we used to.'

Would he never give up? 'Heavens, the meal's scarcely an hour later, Jack,' she said. 'I'm not going to . . . pack in the job. You're being petulant. Surely you can wait three quarters of an hour or so for your dinner in return for sixty pounds a week coming into the house.'

'Less tax' he said.

She closed her eyes. 'Less tax,' she repeated quietly. 'And look what the money's doing. We've a deep freeze already, and I'm going to get an automatic washer this Saturday . . . and we'll have that holiday in France.'

'The garden will do me;' he said; but he accepted the situation after that.

Six months later, on a day when she realised that she did not like the product her firm was making, Laura looked at and listened to her boss more objectively than before as he talked to her at length from his side of the desk.

He had at least one session like this every day when he sat back, and kept glancing at her, often with a look in his eyes, a movement of his lips, which were assessing, daring, which were projecting ideas quite different from what he was talking about.

But she was pretty certain he would never have the courage, thank heavens, to follow up the unspoken enquiries. He would settle for the unhurried therapeutic effect of talking to her, with little smiles, nods, lifts of the eyebrows, caressing his nose, lips and chin between thumb and first finger.

She had only to nod in agreement, give little exclamations of amazement.

She thought, this day, that without doubt, her boss was pompous, complacent, egocentric, cowardly, banal . . . and overpaid . . . as she was. And to think that to listen to such tosh, for being a therapeutic listener to a person she didn't respect, she had exchanged reading Iris Murdoch, she had exchanged appreciating the sensibilities of Saul Bellow, she had exchanged lovely afternoon classes of gentle, civilised, intellectual probing.

When she got home, Jack, who had taken early retirement was whistling in the kitchen as he garnished the meal he had prepared for her. The house and garden were immaculate.

'Did you play bowls today?' she asked wearily.

'Yes, got an hour in,' he said. 'I'm getting better. Then I had a pint. Nice day. Had a good day yourself, love?'

There were times, Laura thought – but it was only a thought – there were times that she thought that she had exchanged the freedom of home for the imprisonment of the office.

16

The Commandos
and the Artist

The six men of a reconnaissance commando unit, one of them injured
and quite ill, were about to leave a hut in which they had sheltered
during torrential rain, when about a quarter of a mile away an enemy
soldier walked into their view, put down a stool, put up an easel, and
looking towards the hut began to paint.

As Captain George Milburn remarked to Sergeant Tom Fintry and
to any of the others who cared to listen: 'That man, a water colourist
probably – incidentally my mother does good water colours – well,
that lone painter makes us six toughies useless.'

'Five,' said Fintry, nodding at the stretcher.

Fintry was so right. Lieutenant Peter Northwood on the stretcher
was now a weakling, not a toughie.

Milburn glanced at his watch. It was two thirty. He looked at Lance
Corporal Lambrook, the medic, kneeling beside Peter; at Corporal
Jenkins staring at his radio equipment, and at Private Mackinnon on
lookout. They all blamed Peter, rightly, for their being in a predicament.
The occasional moan from him evoked annoyance.

Peter, an exuberantly athletic man, that morning, at first light, had
climbed a sloping rock to get a view and had slipped when coming
down. They had heard a bone crack. It had not been essential to clamber
up the rock as two or three hundred yards away the same view could
be seen quite safely from a grassy mound. But for Peter they would not
have been in this hut, and now, for a time, they had lost their freedom
to move about. They were losing time and their presence on the island
was in danger of being known.

Lambrook looked up: 'I might as well ease these straps, sir.'

Milburn nodded, 'And dab some of the sweat off him,' he added.

Mackinnon said in a voice which had some lift to it: 'The sun's
coming out, sir. The clouds are going. The sky's come clear, quickly.
It's like a smashing day on Skye.'

'You can cut the poetry out,' said Fintry, 'and watch if that painter-chappie moves.'

Jenkins said: 'They'll be coming through from the sub in fifteen minutes. All right if I take it out at the back? It'll be better there.'

'As long as you don't take it out more than a yard or two,' said Fintry.

Through his field glasses George Milburn looked at the artist. The man was settled, using his brush fluently, with his left hand.

Milburn turned to Fintry: 'Sarge, check if it's not possible for us to slip away at the back.'

'There's no chance with that rising ground behind, but I'll check,' said Fintry. 'But it's not serious, sir, even if he stays till dark, about six. That is if he stays where he is.'

That was true, thought Milburn: as long as the pinter stayed where he was, and no one else appeared. They would do their last recce that night: an important one at Sandy Bay which was the probable landing place for the assault force.

He'd leave Lambrook behind with Peter. They had fourteen miles to do after that to get back to Hudson Cove, where they were to be picked up by the submarine. Say, with the stretcher, they did a mile an hour, they'd do six or seven miles before dawn, lay up all day, then do the rest nicely by five the following morning, their rendezvous time.

Reassured, Milburn looked again at the artist and thought of his mother painting contentedly among foothills in the Cheviots. She'd be amused when he told her of this.

Mackinnon said: 'I could blow him from here, sir.'

'I'm sure you could,' said Milburn, 'but you're not going to.'

Fintry returned. 'There's no chance of getting out without him seeing us,' he said. 'There's only about ninety yards at the back which he can't see.'

Corporal Jenkins burst into the room. 'Sir,' he shouted.

'Quiet, man,' Milburn snapped.

'Here, this message. It's right. They repeated it. It's right.'

Twenty-four hours had been lopped off. They were to be at their pick-up point at Hudson Cove a day earlier. They had to be there by five the next morning. If they were not there by half five the submarine would leave, and then they had to hide on the island until the assault force came in.

Shocked, Captain George Milburn went cold. All previous cosy plans were blown away. If the worst happened and the man painted on till dark, at about six, that left them with only eleven hours to do the fourteen miles carrying the stretcher in the dark over the rocky up and down coastline. They'd have to dose Peter all right.

And there was still Sandy Bay to recce. He *must* see that. He thought he and Fintry would do it, after six, and catch up the others. But how about if the others lost their way? They could, despite their training, and that would finish things. No, Fintry would have to lead them, and that would also give a four-man lift to the stretcher. He'd recce Sandy Bay on his own.

At four o'clock, with the painter still painting, he told Fintry what he'd decided. Fintry made no comment at first, but a few minutes later said, 'Sir, I think you should be there to guide us. It's a crucial job, everything could hinge on it. It shouldn't be left to someone on the end of a stretcher, likely to get exhausted, if you don't mind me saying so.'

Milburn said, 'It will have to be. I've got to recce Sandy Bay.'

The good thing was that up to Peter's accident they had been on schedule, even though they had spent a fair bit of time checking a long valley and mountain passage direct from Hudson Cove to within three miles of Base One. Base One was name given to the explorers' and scientists' sheds now used by the sixty or so enemy soldiers as their headquarters. Sandy Bay was much nearer to it – only some five miles.

A weak, hoarse voice cried, 'George', and he went to the stretcher. 'Sorry,' Peter muttered. 'Bloody stupid. I know what they'll be thinking. I'm so weak. Scarcely the strength to open my eyes.' In fact his eyes were closed. 'And George, there's all hell let loose in my head.' Milburn sighed, thinking of all the jolting to be endured, and the uncertainty of getting to the pick-up point.

At his vigil at the window he tried to project telepathic messages to the lone figure, suggesting that he had done enough for the day and should go home. Sick of rain, he wished for rain. But the young man just stayed there, absorbed in his painting in the sun.

At five they had their cold rations. Milburn was silent, morose. Now, he was not sure what to do.

At a quarter to six, with the sun sinking, he suddenly said to Fintry, 'I've an uncle who's a journalist and I've heard him say that a complete story which is too late for the deadline is no story, useless, but a three-quarter one which makes the deadline is all right. Well, we'll settle for a ninetenths one. They've cut a day out of our time. We'll omit Sandy Bay.'

Fintry nodded and smiled with relief. 'We've a real chance of getting back, sir, if we leave together.'

People cheered up. Lambrook attended to Peter Northwood gently, tightening the straps carefully, and wry humorous comments were exchanged again. Captain and sergeant studied the route back to Hudson Cove, sometimes lengthening it to avoid rocks and steep places, sometimes shortening by cutting across headlands, and they took bearings in advance.

They would have to average about a mile and a half an hour. They never mentioned that the question of leaving Peter Northwood might arise.

They stood with their packs and personal weapons, and with Northwood securely strapped, but it wasn't until the sun had almost completely disappeared that the painter got up, stretched himself, collected his equipment and walked off the scene. Milburn observed ironically: 'Our friend is going, so we can go.'

They just kept at it throughout that seemingly interminable night slog, pressing on against their pain, and they reached Hudson Cove in time for the rendezvous. Peter Northwood had been unconscious for a long time before he was lifted on to the inflatable dinghy.

On the base ship, after being taken there by the submarine, Milburn was questioned closely. The staff officers would have liked up-to-date information on Sandy Bay, but they weren't critical of his freakish late predicament. Their interest swung to the longer, tougher inland route to Base One.

Milburn asked permission to return with the assault force, and both he and Sergeant Fintry were included, in the role of guides, when the force, some two hundred strong, was landed. They went in at their old place of Hudson Cove, not Sandy Bay, and he and Fintry led them to near Base One by the arduous inland route. Milburn was conscious that if he could have finished his full reconnaissance task, almost certainly they would have had a short and relatively easy journey in from Sandy Bay and have arrived near Base One in good time and fresh.

But, as it was, things went well. At half past three in the morning they surrounded Base One and put over such thundering fire from all sides that the outnumbered and surprised enemy capitulated without a useless fight. The demonstration of fire power was just to shock and impress. The sheds were needed, and the only damage was a chimney stack which crashed through a roof.

When it was all over the captured enemy major asked: 'Why didn't you land at Sandy Bay? It was the obvious place. Perfect. I have so few men, we could wait for you only at one place, so I chose that. My engineering officer went down there every day, planning its defence, painting his water colours while he waited for anti-personnel mines to be parachuted in.

'In the last three days that beach has been sown with mines, and we put in four machine gun positions. We'd have damaged you a lot at Sandy Bay. You would have been in mourning now. We would too, but we would have been defeated with honour. You would not now be giving me a drink, and being superior and smiling. You would have been sad and bitter.'

Milburn fascinated, shocked, thought, Thank God I didn't see Sandy Bay and confirm it as ideal, as almost certainly I would have but for the water colourist.

A little later he said to the enemy major: 'Where is your engineering officer?'

'Been pampered in your hospital. When that chimney fell in, he lost his hand, his painting hand,' the Major laughed.

'His left one,' said Milburn.

'Yes. How clever of you. How did you know?'

'Are his paintings here?' asked Milburn.

'Yes. Take them. Spoils of war,' the Major laughed again.

In the engineering officer's tiny room Milburn soon found the painting he was interested in. Their hut was there all right, the focal point. It was obvious that they would have been seen had they tried to leave.

Back on base ship he visited the hospital ward. Both Peter Northwood and the enemy engineering officer were there.

Peter said: 'I wonder if I should give up climbing.'

'Don't,' said Milburn, 'it got us into the hut.'

The injured water colourist was pale faced and sad looking. After a little while he said: 'Our army does not like artists. In the defence, we have only one injury – to me. I lose my left hand.'

'Our army likes artists,' said Milburn.

The young man made no comment.

'You must learn to paint with your right hand,' said Milburn.

The man closed his eyes and shook his head.

Milburn said: 'Your last painting – the one with the hut, nearly in the centre. I will give you one hundred pounds for it.'

The injured man opened eyes and mouth in astonishment. He smiled wonderfully and said, 'For that you can have them all. And I will learn to paint with my right hand. One hundred pounds. It is a good price you pay.'

Captain George Milburn said: 'It is cheap at the price.'

Edward and His Wife's Infatuation

Edward looked out of their second floor front window – at the blue sea, at the great golden sun, at the brown still fishing vessels, at the high cliffs, and at the people, quietly and seemingly happily, playing miniature golf in the park just below. He looked at couples strolling about, some obviously in love. He had eaten well and soon, with Sheila – his very dear wife – he would go out for a drink to another hotel – nearly as pleasant as this one.

He was very miserable. He wished they had never left home.

He turned and looked at his wife. She was nearly ten years younger, his second wife, and in her late forties she was still a most attractive woman. He loved her now even more than when he had married her three years before. She was looking in the mirror and gently touching and rubbing her cheek bones and under her eyes.

She was – he knew – especially conscious of how she looked at present, because she was infatuated by another man.

Edward closed his eyes and imagined her looking at the other man with that bewildered, lost, withdrawn look of hers and that slight trembling of her lips. The blueness of her eyes seemed to spread under his own eye-lids. God, he hoped this wouldn't be the start of losing her. Ninety-minutes ago – before dinner, before they sat down with the other couple – their mutual loving seemed to be permanent. Now, she would have preferred the other one standing here by the window.

And this man affected him too. He made him less than his usual self, giggly, uncomfortable. In the man's company he used the wrong words, made silly puns. Sheila must have been ashamed of him tonight; seen him as inferior. Yet he felt that he had a finer mind than the other man, but the man was so much at home in the world, relaxed, not trying to prove anything, saying and doing the right things easily at the right time. Especially saying just the right things to Sheila.

Suddenly Edward almost shouted at his wife.

'What do they call them anyway?'

'What do they call who, anyway?' she said quietly.

'Who do you think? That couple we had dinner with.'

'Oh them. Foster. Foster, I'm sure. Kate and . . . and Dick. Kate and Dick Foster.

The name, Dick Foster, he thought, will be causing her to tremble . . . as her name had set him trembling. That man had only to beckon and she'd go to him . . . or him to her, if she beckoned. He sighed as he pictured their meeting: their eyes aglow in their wonderful conspiracy. Then he asked himself: what did he know of his wife? She had been over forty when they met. Her first marriage hadn't lasted ten years, then separation, then divorce. Her husband, she had said, had affairs. Edward wondered how the man could have looked at another woman. If he had had the great good fortune to marry Sheila when she was twenty, he would have known his luck. He wouldn't have strayed in sixty years of marriage . . . But perhaps it was she who had strayed? How could he know what loves, affairs, there had been — especially after that separation? How many lovers?

He gritted his teeth and hammered his right fist into his left palm.

'You picked that up quick,' he said. He felt miserable talking to her like this.

'Picked up what, Edward?' she turned and faced him. 'What are you talking about?'

'Their names, of course.'

'Because I listened. You're not very good at names, you know. They introduced themselves. She brought in his name once, when she was telling that story, and he called her by her name once.' Her voice softened. 'I'd have thought he'd have called her Kathleen or Catherine, wouldn't you?'

'Why should he?'

'Softer names.'

Sadly, he looked out of the window again. 'Kate's all right,' he said.

He must not, he thought, put into words what he had observed, what he knew was happening. Words would make Sheila and he take sides in words. Perhaps, make her admit her feelings for Foster. Perhaps imply previous loves. Words could scar, could rankle. No, he must use his love, his concern, his proximity. And there was the fact of their three happy years together. He could not have been happier than he had been during them. Could she? Had *she* been acting? Had she been pretending that contentment; their loving; her consideration; her protection?

He trembled at the thought. If she had, he did not know her. But keep off words for the present. There could come a time, when distraught, words would pour from him. Then, lost to reason, he would beseech her not to leave him, not to break him, not to take all joy out of his life. He would tell her again of his love, and of his need of her. He would speak of their three years then. He would plead with her to be merciful. He would tell her – it would be true – that he would think of taking his own life. And he would see Foster. He would see Foster first, if it came to words.

And Foster, he thought, he may not want, he may not allow his present life to be destroyed. Not yet anyway. He would start with an affair. After all it seemed that he had been married to Kate for years: that had held and she seemed to be happy enough. No doubt other women had fallen in love with Foster, but the marriage had survived.

Sheila said: 'I said we'd meet them downstairs at half eight.'

He could scarcely talk. 'I see,' he muttered.

She was gazing at herself, touching her hair.

He picked up a newspaper and lay on the bed and opened the paper so that he could not see her.

'I wonder if I should change,' she said.

'I don't,' he began, 'I don't particularly want to go out for a drink with the Fosters.'

They were the first downstairs and when the Fosters arrived – Kate, smiling, chatty; Dick gazing at the elegant, beautiful Sheila – when they were all together Edward was the heartiest of the four.

He suggested the hotel; that they should use his car; he laughed too loud, at his own quips, often inane; he was determined to pay for the first round of drinks and he did so ostentatiously. Midway through the evening Sheila looked at him – with distaste, he thought – and whispered: 'For God's sake, settle down, Edward. Relax.'

And he – sick of himself – allowed, even assisted, the furtherance of their affair. No, he did not feel active enough to do the four-mile walk the next afternoon after the morning coach trip. Kate said she certainly wasn't going on any walk; she wasn't even sure if she'd go on the coach excursion. Sheila's smile became almost permanent and her eyes were bright. She became a little giggly. Dick Foster too, appreciably brightened, not that he had been dull, and with unhurried eloquence he began telling humorous anecdotes, with the cheerful Kate abetting him, reminding him of other incidents. Edward watched Foster's appraisal of Sheila: the smiles which passed between them, the lift of eyebrows. He wanted to denounce Foster, to turn on him a storm of angry words; but he knew he would lose. He knew that Foster would remain calm, look at him intently, speak back well, that he would be reduced to a frustrated whimper, and that Sheila would despise him. And he couldn't just lean across and grab hold of Foster by his lapels and hiss: 'Lay off my wife.' In any case Foster was healthier, stronger, younger.

Back in their room he said: 'Are you sure you're fit enough for that walk?'

'Heavens, it's only four miles, and we've most of the afternoon.'

He dared to say: 'Well, be careful of Foster.'

'Be careful of Foster?' she repeated. 'What do you mean?'

He didn't know what to say, and she went on.

'He'll not push me over the cliffs.'

'No, no, he's more likely to save you,' he said. 'I don't know, Sheila; it's just that he's so sure of himself, in life.'

'But he's not arrogant, overbearing, a loud-mouth, nothing like that. In fact he's modest. He has humility.'

'True, I suppose,' he said, 'True. He's still so sure.' He turned away wanting to finish the unsatisfactory conversation.

'I don't know what you're going on about,' she said, 'and I don't think you do.'

In bed – her back was to him and she was lying near the edge – his toe accidently touched her calf. Her leg twitched and she gasped her irritation. 'Sorry,' he muttered.

The next day the sun beat down. His head and eyes protected by a loose broad-brimmed hat he sat with a paperback and a can of beer at his side and watched the walkers – about a dozen of them – leave for the coastal path. He saw Dick Foster offer Sheila his hat and he heard her laughter of refusal.

Three hours later, sipping tea in the shade, he saw them return. He gave a wry smile and his eyes became moist when he saw – as he had expected – that his wife and Foster were on their own, way behind the others. Then he saw her leave Foster and go into the coach and Foster came on up to him. What was the man going to say to him? Edward sighed in his misery.

'I'm afraid your wife's got a touch of sunstroke,' Foster said. 'I think she needs you. She's in the coach. It's been very hot.'

Sheila looked dreadful. Her face was drained of colour and animation. It seemed longer and thinner, and her cheeks were sunken. She gave a lift of dog-like eyes, pleading for help and comfort. He put an arm round her and drew her to him and she buried her face in his shoulder. 'I think I might be sick,' she whispered. 'I hope I'm not. I feel awful. Edward, I don't want the others around. I don't want him to see me. I've been pretending, but it's no good. I'm so hot . . . yet I'm shivering.'

Her head sunk into his shoulder, her hands gripping his, she moaned and fought with her sickness. He kept wiping her face. The grip of her hands was there all the journey back. He thought she is also frightened of what is happening to her and Foster. She is unsure now; thinking of the disruption of her normal, pleasant life; wondering what the future will be. Nearly everyone in the coach was sorry for her, and Foster came along from his seat and offered a towel and his handkerchief. Edward refused them, saying he was coping, that he thought the worst was over. He felt Sheila's face sink even deeper into his shoulder when she heard Foster's concerned, kind voice.

Sheila was in bed or in their room for three days. The Fosters brought some little present each day. When she came downstairs again and they had dinner with the Fosters, Edward knew that the danger had passed. There was no time now. The Fosters were leaving the next day. The opportunity had gone. Sheila was quiet, reflective. Indeed they all were, with the exception of Kate.

When they did say goodbye Foster and he shook hands; then Foster leant forward and kissed Sheila lightly on the cheek. 'Look after yourself,' he said, looking her straight in the eyes. 'You look refreshed, beautifully refreshed.'

'Thank you,' she murmured. 'I'll be glad to go home.'

He smiled; while Edward said, 'Oh, kissy time,' and he turned to Kate Foster, shining and smiling, and kissed her.

It was some five months later that Sheila said to Edward: 'What did they call that couple we met in Cornwall, dear?'

'Foster. Dick and Kate Foster.'

'What a good memory you have,' she said. 'He was an attractive man, wasn't he? They were both nice. Oh, and wasn't I ill there. That dreadful coach journey.'

'I was grateful for the sun, that holiday,' he said.

'But you, sensibly, wore that big sloppy hat.'

'Yes, you need protection from strong rays, my love. We'll watch it next time.'

'You can say that again,' she said cheerfully.

The Boots

The twin dwarfs began arguing – everyone in the circus could hear them – less than twenty-four hours after their eldest brother, Maurice, had been killed.

The dwarf family, Mrs Dekker and her three sons, had two caravans. Maurice, who had liked privacy now and then, had bought the smaller one.

His body was in there now – in its child's coffin – after he had broken his neck in the ring the night before.

What a tragedy – only thirty years old, so good at his job, so well-liked, such a highly-respected little man.

Maurice had been able to control his younger brothers, with a command he could bring them to heel. Mrs Dekker could too, but she let them go too far, and then sometimes it took so much effort she was left shaking and exhausted.

In the big caravan she watched them now; their faces distorted as they searched for hurting words to scream at each other.

'If he had been here you would not have shouted like this,' she said, shouting herself.

'Well, he's not here,' snapped Arnold.

'I'll live in the little caravan after this,' she stormed. 'I'll not put up with this.'

'Do that,' said Rudolf.

They had squabbled about possessions all their lives. Every time they both wanted the same thing. How many times had they shouted and cried over what Maurice had handed down to them. She said: 'He was here yesterday at this time, and listen to you now.'

Arnold swung round to her, paused a moment to think of his older brother alive at this time yesterday, then finger pointing he darted at her; his finger nearly touched her nose.

'You know, mother, how lovely they are . . . how beautiful, how fine. Rudolf can have all the rest of what Maurice had. Is that not fair?

And was I not born first, one minute before Rudolf? How many times have you told that story? Was I not the second eldest? Am I not now the eldest? They should be mine.'

Rudolf was screaming. Maurice had shown them to him more than to Arnold. He had let him feel them. And how did Arnold know about that minute? Could they tell which was which at the time? Some people couldn't tell now. How could they tell who was first when they were being born? He could have been first.

Rudolf is right, she thought. 'You are *twins*,'' she said.

Arnold stared at her. 'I was born first,' he muttered, 'and they should come to me.'

She gave a sob and the tears flowed a little.

Arnold sighed in annoyance at her distress. She cried rarely. They both went to her slowly, sheepishly, and each put an arm round her. Arnold said gently:

'You must decide for us, little mother.'

'That would mean one of you would hate me.'

'No, no,' they both said; but they were unsure.

Then she said, 'Each of you can have them alternate days.' This was a new thought to them. 'One of you one day, the other the next,' she said. 'Then you both have them. Both my boys, my two remaining boys, have them. We can do this with all his things. No one owns them. The family owns them.'

She rose. 'I'm going in to see him now.'

They watched her go. 'She can't keep away,' said Arnold. Rudolf nodded slowly, and they were quiet, each considering the suggestion of sharing.

In the small caravan Mrs Dekker looked again at the still, set, ashen face of her eldest son, and she talked to him quietly, often sighing in the bewilderment of her sudden grief.

'And you had your brave, sad times too, my son,' she said. 'That time with lovely Ruth . . . and the gift she left you. Remember?' *She* remembered. She knew the story. Maurice, once, had told her everything.

It had been in the summer before last when that beautiful girl, and her tall, thin, sullen, jealous husband Edward, joined the circus. Ruth was not only lovely to look at, she was sweet and kind too. Maurice, two feet shorter than Ruth, lost his heart to her.

He couldn't behave naturally when she was about, and if she gave him a greeting his heart would jump.

28

The husband, Edward – why on earth had she married him? – suspected every grown man of trying to win Ruth's affection – he ignored Maurice, the dwarf. If others looked too long at Ruth or passed some remark about her he would leap towards them, grasping their shirts. Everyone knew that the man was capable of doing injury, even killing.

Then Maurice became aware that Edward had ground for jealousy. Fitz, the daring, athletic Fitz; handsome, arrogant, vain, was also eyeing Ruth a lot. Maurice saw him wink at her, and saw Ruth eventually smile at him, and then she would watch Fitz's dramatic act. All this made Maurice depressed and bitter.

One day Ruth's husband left the circus in his car to go some eighty miles away to pick up some equipment. Ruth was left alone in her caravan. It was the end one, and a copse ran near to it. She had some washing hanging out on a line which stretched from the caravan to a tree, and in the afternoon Maurice saw the figure of Fitz dart from the trees, then behind the washing and into the caravan. That Ruth must have collaborated, had the door waiting open for Fitz, filled Maurice with wonder and envy.

He hit his fist into his hand, he paced about, he was frantic. If only he had been different, and it had been him there now in that caravan and not Fitz. How he would have pleaded with Ruth to run away with him.

Then to his amazement he saw Edward returning, long before he had been expected. The man got out of his car and began to walk smartly down to his caravan.

Maurice experienced a flash of pleasure when he imagined what would happen to Fitz, but then he thought of Ruth; of how she would be shocked, terrified – and what might her madman of a husband do to her?

He leapt into action. He ran to the man, not knowing what he was going to say or do. He grabbed him by the legs, shouting, 'Come to our caravan.' He tried to push the man, 'Come, come to our caravan, please.'

Ruth's husband protested. He scarcely knew Maurice. Maurice said they had something to show him. That his mother had known Edward's father. They had some photographs he must see. He must come in, if only for a minute. And they wanted him to taste some wine.

He pushed and dragged, and eventually the surprised man let himself be taken into their caravan.

Mrs Dekker was in and indeed had thought that she might know the man's father, and that he even might be on a photograph. Maurice got out their box of photographs. He poured out a glass of their best wine, and when Mrs Dekker got over her surprise and began talking to Ruth's husband, Maurice slipped out and hurried to the copse so he could run out of sight down to the end caravan. There he belaboured the door, crying, 'Ruth, Ruth.'

Startled, wide-eyed, she opened the door a little.

'Your husband's here,' he said. 'He's come back early. We're holding him in our caravan, with a drink, but we'll not be able to keep him long.'

Fear struck her face.

'I know Fitz is with you, Ruth,' Maurice said – he had never called her Ruth to her face before – 'that's why I've come. That's why I stopped Edward coming straight down.'

He ran back into the copse, back to the big caravan and as he leant against it, struggling to get his breath, he saw Fitz saunter into his own caravan, and a moment later Edward left theirs.

Ruth took such notice of Maurice after that. She was very grateful. She would smile when she caught his eye, speak to him softly, pat him on the head and often finger his hair as she went by, sending tremors of delight through him.

Then she invited him to have tea with her.

She said there would have been a terrible scene if Edward had found Fitz in the caravan; that there would have been violence. All her life she would be grateful to Maurice for preventing that happening, for being so clever, so brave, so concerned, so unselfish. She said she wanted to reward him, to give him a present. Anything. Anything he wanted. What would he like? What did he want?

And she smiled as she said: 'You do watch me, Maurice . . . all the time. I've noticed.'

'I can't help it,' he said. 'You're so lovely. If I were like Fitz I would run away with you . . . if you would let me.'

Ruth stretched out a hand and took hold of his.

'Poor Maurice,' she said. 'No wife, no girl.'

He shook his head.

'Ask anything of me,' she said, 'anything . . . and you shall have it.'

He flushed. He could scarcely believe what he thought she was offering.

'Beautiful, Ruth,' he murmured.

She nodded. 'Just ask . . . for what you want,' she said. 'There will be a time, when I can give it.'

'If you . . . if we . . .' he began, and then there was the sound of whistling as someone walked by outside. Ruth looked round, out of the window, and gazed at the tall handsome figure of Fitz.

When she turned back to Maurice her look and voice were changed. Her eyes had lost their brightness, her face was sad.

Maurice was bent forward, still searching for words to ask if she would love him, for half an hour, for five minutes, then, as he saw she had lost interest in him, he stopped trying for the words. When she forced herself to look at him he saw a sudden distaste in her face, a little revulsion, fear, regret. She flushed and trembled.

'Yes?' She spoke in a voice gone dull, hard, as if she were speaking to a stranger. His heart dropped. He paused, then said quietly:

'What I would like, would love, if you could get them for me, is a pair of boots, specially made for me. I would love a pair of good boots which fitted me properly. I have to wear children's boots, you know,' and he kicked his leg forward.

She gazed at him, and smiled, then she leant forward and kissed him on the forehead.

'Bless you, Maurice,' she said, 'you are a very good friend . . . a true friend. I will get you the best pair of boots you have ever seen. We will find out who is the best bootmaker, and you shall go to him.'

And Maurice did. The boots he got were a joy; splendid to look at, a pleasure to feel, and his feet were so happy in them.

The boots were there now, below the coffin. Mrs Dekker picked them up and stroked them. These were what the twins were quarrelling over – the best pair of dwarf's boots the family had ever seen.

When she went back into the big caravan Arnold asked her who would wear the boots for the first day? He thought he should. Rudolf said they would cut cards for it.

Then the twins had an argument about using cards, and thought of turning a domino, flipping a coin, throwing dice. They seemed to favour throwing dice.

Before the funeral the next day Arnold and Rudolf ran out of the small caravan each wearing one of the boots. They called to her, asking how they looked, and each told her what a good fit his boot was.

'Take them off,' she ordered, 'Take them off.' Then they asked why couldn't they throw the dice now so the boots could be worn straightaway?

'Let him be buried first,' she said. 'And wait till we have left this cursed place. At the next place, we can make a fresh start.'

Grumbling, they agreed.

'I will keep the boots,' she said.

Before the coffin lid was screwed down, she went yet again to look at her eldest son.

'How many times must she look at him?' said Arnold. '*Was he not her favourite.*'

So Maurice was buried, and the circus moved away. When they got to their new place, the twins, in a day of great tension, threw the dice. Then Arnold said:

'Have you the boots, little mother?'

'I know where they are,' she replied.

'I wear them first,' he said.

She shook her head. 'You will never wear them, neither will you, Rudolf. The boots are with Maurice for ever more. I put them in the coffin beside him.'

A Lunchtime
News Item

I heard the news at lunchtime, on regional television. My friend James Devine had been killed in a car accident on Hartside Pass in the Pennines. I straightaway phoned Delia, his wife, with whom I was in love, and after a few words suggested that I should come round to help her.

She said, 'That may not be wise.' I thrilled at the implication that she thought others would or could think that there was a serious relationship between us and would disapprove of my presence at this time.

'I'll be about only when I'm of use,' I said. 'And I was his friend, perhaps his closest.'

'Yes . . . of course. Yes, come round, Colin, there are matters you can help me with.'

I was relieved about that. Although I had known her and been in love with her for ten years, since before she met James, in the days when he and Jennifer, his twin sister, seemed to be inseparable, I was still uncertain how she would react. It was only after her marriage and when I became fairly successful and confident that I made an impression. We were old friends now, and she knew how I felt, of course. After many years of unwavering, and unrequited, love for her, I determined to be careful. I did not want to spoil this opportunity, so tragically presented.

I had liked James. We had played a weekly game of golf together for years. Relaxing and enjoyable times. Bouts of talk, spells of quietness. No desire to score over each other. Seeing him, in my mind's eye, on the golf course, I felt devastated.

Two things came to me as I drove round to see Delia. First, had she let Jennifer know? It was possible that she hadn't. They hadn't spoken to each other, I knew, for more than eight years, since it became obvious that James was going to marry Delia. It was Jennifer, of course, who had made the break. I assumed that she would come down for the funeral from Scotland.

Jennifer left home when the preparations for the wedding really got under way and went up to Edinburgh at first. She never returned, not for the wedding, not for the briefest visit. Within a year of leaving, she, who never had a steady boy friend in the north east, was married – to a doctor with a country practice in Inverness-shire.

Although there was no doubt that the twins had been totally estranged for a year or two, I was pretty sure in myself that they had been seeing each other in recent years. I remembered references to Jennifer, and to Edinburgh, realised that Edinburgh was about equidistance between Newcastle and Inverness, and it became clear to me that it was highly likely that the twins met there.

The second thing which appeared to me to be important followed my thinking about what could have happened to James on Hartside. The Pass could be a devil in winter, but this was a clear spring day. James could have been going too fast; he could have been avoiding another car, or a sheep. Something could have gone wrong with the car. He could have had a heart attack: even though he was only in his early forties.

And then came a further possibility – a startling one. I remembered him saying to me, 'I don't suppose you have any enemies?'

'Only myself,' I'd replied, thinking of the misery, the waste of years, my feeling for his wife had caused me.

'I've some real enemies,' he said. 'People who would like to see me out of it, that is out of my business, failing that, dead. There are one or two who'd like to run me off the road.'

It was that phrase: 'run me off the road' which zoomed in on me. Was it just a metaphor, or had it to be taken literally? Where had he been going this morning? If he'd been going to a conference in Manchester, or Liverpool, others would know, and they could well know his preferred route via Alston and Hartside.

I arrived at the detached mid-nineteenth century mansion, now occupied by Delia alone. Delia's car was in the gravelled drive. In my mind's eye I saw James leaving those high strong shining doors early that very morning. The house had been left to him by his parents along with other property and investments. With his own successful business there was no shortage of money.

A woman neighbour friend of Delia's opened the door and whispered that Delia was brave and that it was kind of me to offer to help. Delia's face was paler than I had ever seen it. Her eyes were big and staring, almost as if she wasn't seeing. She was trembling.

She told me that James had left about eight for a meeting in Manchester. The accident had happened at nine.

'I'd be having coffee and toast then,' she said. 'I didn't feel anything. I always thought I would, if something like this happened.'

'You've let Jennifer know?' I asked.

'No,' she said.

'Friends who've heard it on the news might ring her.'

'I can't speak to her. There's a blockage there now.'

'I'll ring her.' I said. 'I'll do that first.'

'I haven't the number.'

'I'll get it from enquiries,' I said. As I listened to the ringing Delia said, 'I've never spoken to her since the days when James and I were courting.'

The doctor husband answered. He said Jennifer was out, but that she shouldn't be long as he had expected her in for lunch.

'I never met him,' he said when I told him of James. 'And I'm very sorry. And Jennifer will take it hard, I fear. She often talked of him. It's a shame there was this separation within the family – terrible, unnecessary and stupid, I thought, and now it's too late. But I was involved only on the periphery, you might say. Yes, of course, we'll come down. I'll make arrangements so that I can bring her.'

I liked the sound of the doctor-husband.

Delia said her parents would be coming and staying, implying that it would be difficult to put up Jennifer and her husband. I didn't make the point that this was the house in which Jennifer had been brought up.

'Of course she'll take it hard,' she said bitterly. 'It wasn't a success, you know – our marriage. This is a family house, but there's no family. He wasn't the greatest of lovers, I'm afraid.'

Why was she speaking against him? I supposed it was the mention of Jennifer which was affecting her.

'If it could have continued the way it started. The first two years or so were good. We should have had children then. We could have had. But, eventually, that separation from Jennifer told, spoiled his life. I loved him for a long time. I wasn't to blame. I was faithful to him. *You* should know that. I did my best, and failed. He had long morose periods. Lost in thought, sighing. I once yelled at him: 'Go and live with her.' I think it was the only time I raised my voice to him. And you know what, you know what happened? – he cried.'

'That's where his heart was – up in Scotland. Speak to the police and check that he was alone, will you.'

'They'd have told you if he wasn't, Delia.'

'Yes, yes,' she said. 'Sorry. I can't think straight when I think of her. . . . Colin, would you formally identify him? Would you do that for me? Would you go over to Carlisle, love, they've taken him there, and do that for me? D'you mind?'

'All right.'

'How do you think it happened?' I said.

'It's odd he went over at speed.' Delia said. 'He's never had an accident all the time I've known him.'

'How about if he'd been run off the road by someone. You know he had enemies?'

'Yes, I do, but I don't think they'd do anything like that . . . would they?'

'He once told me he had real enemies. That one or two would like to run him off the road. That was his phrase. Maybe someone did that this morning. Bumped him, forced him over an edge.'

She leant forward and grasped my hands.

'I wish it were that.'

'Why?' I asked. She smiled weakly, and then she dismissed an explanation. 'But I can't believe it. They didn't mention any other car. But tell the police – what James told you.' She got up and walked about. 'It would make it easier for me if it were that. And it is possible.'

'Delia,' I exclaimed, 'you're saying it would make it easier for you if he'd been murdered.'

'He's gone, so better like that,' she said. 'Will you attend the inquest with me, and tell them what he said to you?'

'Yes,' I said, puzzled. My puzzlement was soon cleared as the phone rang and she indicated that she didn't want to answer it.

It was the Scottish doctor. I listened and listened, wondering if I was hearing right. 'I'm terribly sorry,' I said. 'This has been a dreadful day.'

'Now, did you get the time of James's accident?' the doctor asked.

'Yes, rather definite, nine o'clock.'

'Nine o'clock,' he repeated. 'The same time. Oh, my Jennifer. No, not mine.' Then he added, 'I'll live. I'll get a life going,' and he put down the receiver.

Delia said, 'I know what you're going to say. We can forget any other car, can't we.'

'I think so. Jennifer's dead. She died this morning. A car accident, at the same time. On her own. Her car went over an edge in the

Cairngorms.'

Delia pressed her hand over her mouth, and ran out of the room.

I phoned Carlisle and eventually agreed to be over there between half past nine and ten the next morning to formally identify the body. The postmortem was to be carried out later in the morning. They told me that no other car was involved, and that James's car had been seen going over an edge, as if being driven over. I told them about Jennifer – I thought they ought to know.

Delia came back into the room. 'They could have had heart attacks at the same moment. They could each have had a feeling that they had to go into the hills. Is that possible? Could there have been a sort of unconscious telepathy between them?'

'Maybe. I don't know.'

'To do the same thing at the same time, I mean, without being aware. Better than a pact, a suicide pact.'

'We'll know more tomorrow, after the postmortems,' I said.

'A heart attack at the same time. That's what I hope now. I couldn't win, could I. Nor could that doctor up there. We should never have tried to come between them. But pact or a heart attack, makes no difference, really does it. Shows how they were inseparable.'

I nodded.

'Poor James. But, for me, it was . . . unsatisfactory. . . . Colin!'

'Yes.'

'How about insurances? Will you glance at his policies and see if they're affected if it's suicide. Although I'm sure I'll be well provided for. James was good that way.'

I followed her into James's study and waited as she pulled out drawers and looked at papers. I could see that Delia would live too. Like the Scottish doctor she had done her best. Yes, she would get a life going too. With me, probably, but not certainly. She would always carry with her an understandable resentment against James, and Jennifer. I wouldn't. I felt I'd be saddened all my life by their deprivation and their end.

Vice Versa

A short, dark-haired, well-dressed man, pleasantly confident and mannered, nicely at home in the world, walked leisurely from his club, juggling with the merits of a number of restaurants.

There had been rain and the air was soft. There was just an occasional minor fluster of drizzle, not enough to cause the man to unfurl his umbrella. Reflected city lights glistened on the damp pavements.

The man had enjoyed his aperitif at the club and the company, and, as often happened, he had enthralled them with his tales. They had not known whether or not to believe him.

He passed a tramp sitting within the columned entrance of an office block on the higher and dry steps. The tramp, tall, fair-haired, was intent on peeling an orange.

The affluent man stopped some twenty yards past the tramp and sighed. An aspect, completely different from that of a moment before, came over his face. He closed his eyes and bent his head. Then he walked back, stood before the tramp and taking two pound coins out of his pocket proffered them to the man.

The tramp looked up, both men smiled, the tramp took the coins, the men nodded to each other, and the rich one resumed his stroll to his restaurant.

A week later the rich man again saw the tall, fair-haired tramp sitting on the steps with his head down, although he wasn't peeling an orange this time. The rich man's sigh was deeper and before he went to his appreciated dinner he gave the tramp five pounds.

Again the men did not speak, just smiled and nodded. They were about the same age and an observer could have thought this was the bond between them – that they had known the same span of years.

The short, dark-haired man was a man of habit and most nights of the week he walked down the same street past the steps. He didn't see the tramp until a month later.

He had decided what he would do if he saw the man again, but even so he had his habitual ponder before he went back and handed the man fifty pounds, in five-pound notes and coins.

Three months passed, winter was nearly over, when the rich man noticed the tramp again on the steps. He had been watching for him but his heart nearly stopped when he did see him. He gasped as if he was going to cry, and walked on quickly. He walked to near the luxurious restaurant he had intended to enter. He gazed into a lighted shop window to make it less easy for people to notice his torment.

When he turned away he went, not into the restaurant, but into a snack bar. He moved some dirty crockery to one side, and after cleaning a place with a paper bag, he got out his bank statement and cheque book, made some calculations, and then wrote out a cheque for £19,867.

He didn't even buy a cup of tea but walked straight back to the tramp and handed him the cheque.

The tramp got up. He was very thin. Feeling for his glasses he took the cheque to the light of a lamp. The short stocky man followed him.

'Under twenty thousand, I see,' observed the tramp.

'Yes.'

The tramp nodded and said, 'You are so kind, so kind.'

'No doubt you are kind too . . . in your turn.'

'I have been so.'

'Here are my keys.'

'Thank you.'

'The winter, at any rate, is nearly over.'

'Yes. I know all about it. You have my heartfelt good wishes.'

Ten months later a tall, fair-haired, well-dressed man, pleasantly confident and mannered, nicely at home in the world, strolled down the same street on his way from his club to a select restaurant.

He noticed a short, dark-haired tramp resting on the higher steps within the columned entrance of an office block. The tall, fair-haired, affluent man walked on, then paused, closed his eyes and shivered.

He turned and went back to the short, dark-haired man – who hadn't looked up – and profferred him two pounds.

The Brave Call
of Mrs Tucker

Suddenly, without making a mental decision, Mrs Tucker pushed herself away from the stone balustrade overlooking the sea and began walking towards the house.

It might be better this way, she thought; almost before I know what I'm doing I'll have pressed the bell and I'll be seeing her.

It was the fifth time she had approached the house in the last two hours. She tried to walk normally but weakness was sprouting in her legs, and her head got tilted sideways.

The house was imposing: three-storied, brown rough stone, big windows with casement curtains, the door set inside a columned entrance. She knew the girl, Marilyn lived on the second floor with another girl student.

The door was some twenty yards away across a forecourt of grass and a wide curving cement path and she was just about to push the gate when the door opened and two men came out. One was obviously about to leave, but the two men stood and talked.

Mrs Tucker hesitated. It would be awkward to go in now, in front of those men. To have to stand by them and ring the bell as they were talking. . . . She had better call back. It wouldn't be quite polite to stand there. She could easily call back again.

She turned away and walked round a corner into a side street of shops. Her pace slowed. She felt heavy with despair. She stopped and looked in a shop window. She had already examined the prices an hour before.

Her reflection didn't cheer her. A chubby middle-aged woman, thickish legs, skirt too short, coat too bulky, her face pale and woeful, topped by a sloping column of hair elongated by an enormous black hair-piece.

Other women, she thought, confident, educated women, oh, so at home in the world, would have been in that house, talked to the girl, and been back home by now.

Well, she wasn't like them. She had to make the best of what she was. Olive Tucker, who had left school at fifteen, married when she was twenty to a dreamer of a man whom she seemed to know less and less. She'd had three children, and the eldest, Bob, was at university.

And he was miserable, over this girl Marilyn, so very miserable that she was alarmed. She was worried at what he might do.

She wanted to see the girl and tell her – but Marilyn was educated; and she was Olive Tucker, who had a part-time job in a fruit shop. But she got on with people. People liked her. . . . She wasn't even sure if she should be here.

She gave a little nod to her reflection: 'How d'you do. Not so well, eh? You're not really frightened of a twenty year old, are you? She's only a lass, after all. Have a coffee, love. Have what you fancy.'

She went back to the sea-front into a little cafe and looked out at the sea as she stirred her coffee. There were a few striding people on the beach, some circling dogs, rows of dark seaweed; and a pier and a thin breakwater swept away out to sea until they were lost in the mist. At the corner of the pier and the lower promenade the sand was humped into dunes and there was some grass there. Grass will grow anywhere, she thought.

The foghorn moaned. It had been doing that for two hours. Like a dog in pain.

Sipping the coffee she felt again the reasons for her fright. She was scared the girl, Marilyn, would humble her with words, and that the girl would really have no patience with her.

Then, should she be here at all? Was she not interfering? Of course she was. Of course she was. She was going to see this girl, whom she had never met, Bob's girl friend for a year – girl friend, that was putting it mildly – she was going to tell her how Bob was.

Did Marilyn know what she had done to him? Bob was quiet, like his father, and he didn't find it easy to get on with people – even though he was educated. Perhaps it was the way he dressed. He had been dependent on that girl. To drop a boy like Bob so completely was cruel. And she had got him used to a woman, Marilyn had. Mrs Tucker didn't want to think of details.

She couldn't think sensibly about it now, she knew that. It had become an issue of bravery, or cowardice.

A young man, long hair and beard, wearing an old duffle coat came into the cafe. For a moment she thought he was Bob and she felt an uprush of terror. How Bob would have stood transfixed and stared, then marched across and almost shouted at her:

'What are you doing here? You never come here. You're not here to see Marilyn, are you? You are, you've come to see Marilyn. You haven't seen her, have you? How dare you? How dare you? Why, why, why, can't you just keep to what you know? Oh, mother.'

And he would sink down on the chair opposite and shake his head and sigh.

Him and his pride. The girl might dash off straightaway to see him. Mrs Tucker stood up. Young people, she thought, when they were floundering were sometimes relieved to have interfering help.

She was going to see Marilyn now. There could be a football team at the door, they wouldn't stop her.

At the gate there was an old sports car and a young man working on it – his head inside the bonnet. There was no one at the door. She rang the bell for the second floor. She heard a door bang, someone thumping and running downstairs, and a girl's voice rang out gaily, 'Coming.'

The door jerked open and a tall girl, with the shortest of minis at the top of her long legs looked down at her. The girl's face fell from gay welcome into dismay. 'Oh,' she exclaimed in a little voice.

'Marilyn?' Mrs Tucker asked.

'No, no; I'll get her.'

The girl came out on to the step and shouted at the busy young man, 'How long you going to be?' She closed the door before the boy could extricate his head, and gazed at Mrs Tucker: 'Shall I tell her who it is?'

'Mrs Tucker.'

'Oh. Oh.' The girl was alarmed. 'I'll tell her.' She started to run upstairs, then looked back, doubtful about leaving Mrs Tucker in the hallway. Halfway up the first flight of stairs, she yelled, 'Marilyn.'

'Yes.' It was a soft voice. Mrs Tucker could just hear it.

'Mrs Tucker's here to see you.'

There was a pause, then a tentative: 'Who, Marj?'

'Mrs Tucker.'

'Bob's mother?' Mrs Tucker felt, rather than heard the fearful enquiry.

'I think so.' Marj glanced back at Mrs Tucker, who nodded.

There was another pause, then the voice said: 'I'll come down.'

Mrs Tucker waited, watching the stairs. She could not get out of it now.

'Hello, Mrs Tucker.'

The voice came first, before she saw the girl.

A small girl with big dark eyes, and so pretty, oh, so pretty. Mrs Tucker swallowed hard at the thought, at the new understanding of her son's distress. The girl looked straight at her, gave her a little smile and held out her hand.

'Will you come upstairs.'

She followed Marilyn upstairs into a large room overlooking the sea. Some wall cloths and some weird paintings made her uneasy.

'It's about Bob?' the girl asked.

'Yes: I'm worried about him. He's very miserable.'

'I'm sorry,' the girl's voice was unsteady.

'I don't know what to do about him, really' Mrs Tucker said.

'He hasn't gone back home, has he? He's not with you, now?'

'No, he's still in his flat. He won't give that up . . . as long as he can pay the rent.'

'Does he know you're here?' the girl's eyes widened.

'No. . . . Won't you see him?'

The girl shook her head.

Mrs Tucker said: 'But, it's because of you, you know. He's got used to you. He . . . he thinks a lot about you. He's not one for making a lot of friends, as you know. I don't think he's ever had a girl friend, really, before you.'

'He should have had, Mrs Tucker. I shouldn't have been the first, and he shouldn't think I'm the last. There's Marj thinks he's super, and he never took any notice of her.'

'She liked him?' It was Mrs Tucker's turn to be somewhat incredulous.

'Yes. I'm sorry, Mrs Tucker, but he must manage without me. It'll be better for him.'

Marj brought in the tea then: 'Here, you pour,' she said to Marilyn. 'I'm going.'

'He couldn't be just a friend if I went back, and that's all I can be now' Marilyn said.

Mrs Tucker was aware she was beginning to blush.

'He has to get over it . . . and he will,' the girl said.

'I wish I could be sure,' Mrs Tucker said.

'Bob's too sensible to do anything really silly. He is, Mrs Tucker.'

'You think so? You think so?'

'Yes.'

Relief flowed slowly through Mrs Tucker and a weight was lifted from her. For the first time in her life she was admitting that there was someone who knew more about Bob than she did. She accepted Marilyn's assurance as coming from inner realms denied to her.

'He must make new friends,' Marilyn was saying; 'join a society or two. He'll do that, in time. He has plenty of interests.'

'He'd look after you,' Mrs Tucker said quietly.

'Too much. I don't want to be looked after yet. He ties me down; restricts, confines. Bob's very possessive, Mrs Tucker . . . jealous.'

Mrs Tucker nodded. She could believe it.

'When I left him at the end,' the girl said, 'it was like bursting into the fresh air. . . . I'm still relieved.'

'Oh, my,' Mrs Tucker exclaimed, shocked, saddened.

'I loved him,' the girl went on, 'I think I did. I'll always be concerned about him. Maybe in three or four years' time – I don't know. . . . He may change. I may feel differently.'

Mrs Tucker rose, 'I might as well go,' she said.

'Bob knows he has to work it out himself,' Marilyn said. 'I'll come with you to the bus stop, Mrs Tucker.'

'No, no; it's all right.'

'I'd rather.'

Mrs Tucker put out a hand to restrain the girl a moment from getting up.

'You really think he won't do anything silly?'

'I'm certain he won't. I'll get my coat.'

Mrs Tucker watched the girl stretch for her coat. She would have liked her for a daughter-in-law.

She wasn't sure what they chatted about on the way to the bus stop, but when they waited there she was enveloped by despondency. She had failed. And she felt unbelief again that this girl, this nice girl – no matter how close she had been with Bob – this nice educated girl could be so stubborn, so hard.

'I find it hard to believe you won't see him,' she said. 'He is in need of help . . . and you were so close.'

'No, no,' the girl shook her head slowly. 'I'm sorry, Mrs Tucker. I couldn't. I am finished . . . for the time being, at any rate. It's better for both of us this way.'

On the journey home, Mrs Tucker thought she would see what she could do for Bob in that flat. She would encourage him to get out; meet another girl – she had never thought she would do that. She wished she could tell him that a girl like Marj thought he was super.

She would say: 'Come back home for awhile, any time you feel like it, for a change.' He would mutter something, be impatient. But later he might appear and say he was coming back for a few weeks. You never know.

She would be ready to help him in any way she could. Any way that *he* wanted, whether he told her so or not. What *she* wanted didn't matter.

That was as much as she could do. Oddly, she didn't feel too unhappy. She knew more about people. She was glad she had made the call.

The Anniversary

Except for the lone figure the town looked to be sleeping, as well it should at two o'clock in the morning of a cold windy night.

The figure was that of a tall thin man in a long black coat, his face hidden within upturned collar and turned-down hat. He was keeping in to the railings coming down Cemetery Road and when he came to shops and houses he kept close to the windows and walls. He was bent into the wind and he swayed at times, but he pressed on.

Such a man, one felt, would be just as intent and withdrawn in crowded daylight.

Some two miles away in the town the wind kept an elderly couple awake. The man hoped that this would mean he would sleep-in the next morning so that an hour or so of a dreaded anniversary would be lost to his consciousness. His wife, he knew, would be up at her usual early hour, and her face and voice would never allow him to forget what day it was.

They had managed the previous day not to mention the anniversary. A considerate couple they had spoken only when a remark was necessary, not risking chatter in case it led them to talk of their son.

Now they intermittently sighed, moved and turned over. The wind howling, rushing, moaning, was alien and merciless. Its sound tore at them, crying and wailing.

At last she spoke. He knew when she jerked her face clear of the clothes that their silence was over.

'You shouldn't have written that letter,' she said.

He delayed replying, but eventually he said, 'Try to sleep.'

'You shouldn't have written it the way you did.'

'Please, please.'

'He'd have been alive now.'

'Please, Meg.'

'My boy.'

'*Our* boy'

Slowly she accepted this. 'A year ago. Our boy,' she said.

But now he raised himself on an elbow. 'He wasn't a child. He wasn't a boy. He was a grown man with an important job. And you must stop blaming me. I'm not strong enough to bear it, and it's unfair. I wouldn't have written but for you. You moaned on, more than me, about him not coming to see us. He hadn't been for months, and he only lived at the other end of the town. There were days when you mentioned that three or four times.'

He was unhappy at speaking out against his son, Colin, but he needed the support of truth, of how it had been.

'And he had his car,' he said.

'That. I wish to God he hadn't.'

He went on, rushing on now to divest himself of the guilt she had thrown on him.

'You saw the letter. I read it out to you. I'd have altered it if you'd said. You said it was all right; it would do.'

'I never liked it.'

She turned her face into the pillow.

He said, 'He shouldn't have got into such a state, just because we said it was time he paid us a visit. Should he? We've only Gavin's word that he got into a state, anyway, haven't we? And you can't rely on a man like that. His friend. We just wanted him to look us up. We weren't trying to alter his life.'

She lifted her head. 'You're wrong there,' she said, 'we were, if the truth be known. You're not right all the time.'

He lay back. He knew she was right.

'Why couldn't we have left him alone,' she said. 'Let him live the way he wanted to. He had a right to that. He wasn't hurting anybody — except what we thought. Old foggies. A grown man. If he wanted . . . to be with . . .'

'Gavin,' he supplied.

'. . . it was no business of ours.'

'All the same, he could have looked us up now and again,' he said, 'that's all. Didn't take much effort. We didn't ask for much.'

'We should be shot,' she said, 'old people like us. Only thinking of ourselves. Wanting attention. Why should we have attention? We've had our time. He'd have come round. Putting pressure on him. And they weren't behaving right to him at work. He was good at heart. He could always get worked up easily. That's why he had the accident on the way.'

He stroked her arm. 'A tragedy, that's what it was,' he said. 'Meg; Meg, perhaps we should see Gavin. Eh? For Colin's sake. Shall we try tomorrow? Something definite, instead of just brooding here.'

'He hates us. He blames us, for interfering, for badgering. He knew we didn't like it. And you say he's half round the bend, don't you.'

'He is; but he cared. He was the only one besides us who really cared.'

'I wish tomorrow was over,' she said. Then she began to tremble, and sobbing managed to say that she was sorry that she had blamed him. He nestled into her back and put an arm round her.

They were still in the shallows of sleep when a sound struck through them.

It was the letter box flap downstairs being dropped. Although not louder than the wind the sound was metallically clear and sharp.

They lay still. The old man knew it couldn't be the wind lifting the flap. The flap was too heavy. Who, what, at time of night? Could it be a lost, despairing dog?

He hoped it would not happen again. But . . . it fell again, re-sounding within him. There was no doubting it. Surely, surely, no one would be pushing things through at such an hour, on such a night. He felt someone was there. Fear swelled, then surged through him. Had he to get up and go to the door?

He whispered, 'Meg, did you hear that?'

'Yes,' she said and she sat up and grasped his arm. 'And you know who always did that – never knocked properly – Colin.'

He knew. He lay, mouth open a little.

'I'll get up if it goes again,' he said. 'I'll have to.'

He hadn't long to wait. It fell again. 'Oh,' he moaned and he swung his legs out of bed and shivering, sought his slippers.

'It's half past two,' he said, reaching for his dressing gown.

'Look out of the window first,' she said.

He went to the window and drawing the curtain a little looked down. He went cold with fear. There was a man there, a tall thin man in a long black coat. He looked like Colin, and then aware of the moved curtain the man looked up and said something. Little of the face was visible in the dim light between collar and hat but he seemed to say: 'Here I am, father.'

The old man staggered away, as if thrust back.

'Who is it? What is it?' his wife cried.

'My God,' he muttered, collapsing on the bed.

'It's Colin, isn't it,' she said, and lifting the bedclothes from her she was across the room and at the window in seconds. 'It's him. Colin.'

The man below stared up at her and spoke. She thought he said: 'I've come to see you, mother.'

'He's not dead,' she cried, and she made for the bedroom door, squeezing past her husband sitting head down on the bed. He grasped her nightgown but it slipped out of his fingers.

'Woman,' he said, 'stop,' but she was running down the stairs. He caught her in the passage before she could open the door and pressed her against the wall.

'It can't be Colin. Understand, Meg. It's not, Colin. We saw him . . . bandaged . . . in that chapel place. I identified him. Stop shaking your head. He's dead, killed in that accident.'

'That's Colin, at the other side of the door,' she said. 'I know my own son. There's mistakes. It might never have happened. Let me go.'

But he held her.

'He's come home,' she cried. 'How dare you . . . stopping me.'

Hearing the door flap being lifted again they turned and saw the finger tips of leather gloves.

'His gloves,' she breathed. 'We bought them.'

The flap fell with a noise which seemed to press through their bodies making them cringe.

'You must let him in. You must open the door – even if it's not Colin. But you know it is . . . in your heart.'

'Meg, I'm lost; I'm afeared.'

'Frightened. You're frightened . . . of Colin. Colin,' she called. 'Colin. Wait. We'll open up.'

'All right,' he said, relaxing his hold, 'I'll do it, if you go back upstairs. If it's Colin . . . the Colin we knew, I'll bring him up to you.'

She knew he would. He was a man of his word. 'Open the door,' she said, 'now,' and ran upstairs.

The old man turned to the door. He breathed deeply, pulling back his shoulders. What would he see? He was prepared to die of fright. He moved back the bolt. 'Yes, yes,' he said, and pulled the door open, holding it against the wind.

There was no one there, or there seemed to be no one in the shifting shadows. Dismissing the temptation to force the door shut again, he stepped outside, and there walking away head down, was the man who had stood at the door.

He called out: 'Come back. Don't go. Colin.'

The figure did not look back, and was soon lost in stretches of deeper blackness. Should he follow, and find out? She might expect that. No, that was beyond him. He had done his bit. Slowly he closed and locked the door and rubbed his chest to try to ease the thumping and the pain of his heart. He was miserable and began to shiver uncontrollably. He pulled himself upstairs.

His wife said: 'I saw him leave. You should have let me open the door. He couldn't bear being kept waiting . . . and on such a night. But, he should have waited a little longer . . . after all . . .'

'He went when he heard me unlocking the door,' he said. 'but it wasn't Colin. It was Gavin, that madman, his friend. Gavin, getting his own back on us. Hurting us more. Working out his hate, and his pain. He's demented – like we are at times.'

'He'll come again . . . Colin,' she said. She got into bed. 'Come to bed. You'll be ill tomorrow. You're shivering. It's all right. He'll be back. We'll not keep him waiting next time.' She pulled the bedclothes tightly round him, then she hugged him.

After a minute or so, when his breathing had become more normal, she said, 'Next year, for the anniversary – if we're still living – we'll not lock the door. We'll leave it just open, so he can come straight in. We'll do that, eh? That'll be best.'

'Yes,' he said, 'we'll do that. Let come in, whoever wants to come in.'

The Kneeling Woman

When the doorbell rang Eva was sure it would be Lloyd although it was early for him. Her mother's hands began to shake on the upholstered arm of the big chair and her eyes showed alarm and resentment.

'It's all right,' said Eva, smiling. Then she said clearly to the deaf, near helpless woman who stared at her lips, 'It will only be Lloyd.'

'Lloyd, Lloyd,' her mother's lips and chins began to quiver. 'He's coming too early that man. I don't know why he comes.'

It *was* Lloyd at the door, boyish for his forty years. And perhaps she was girlish for her thirty-eight. She was slim, lithe, graceful.

'Eva,' he breathed, 'Eva'. As she held the door his hand searched for her free hand. She lifted it away before his grip could tighten. 'Lloyd,' she said. 'You are early How nice. We'll have longer together.'

He followed her down the passage trying for her hand again, but failing. 'I want to talk to you about that, Eva.'

'About what?' she said when they were in the living room. 'Say hello to mother.'

Lloyd turned and spoke carefully. 'Hello, Mrs Hargreaves. I hope you are feeling better. I hope you have had a better day. I came early tonight.'

Mrs Hargreaves looked at him for a few seconds then at her daughter. 'He's early,' she said. 'I'll be wanting to go to the . . .'

'Yes, yes, mother,' Eva said. 'Don't worry. Settle down again. I'll take you.' She spun round to smile at Lloyd, 'Lloyd, what were you wanting to talk to me about?'

'About being together, longer. Eva, about being together always. I've been thinking.' He moved nearer and raised his hands to hold hers but she put her hands behind her back. She stood facing him, rocking slightly on her heels, smiling, the pleasure of his arrival gone flat a little.

'Good,' she said, playing for time and turning away to the kitchen door. 'I like your visits. Life wouldn't be so good without them.'

'It seems a pretty poor life to me, Eva,' he said, 'what you have. But, by God, you do your duty by your mother. You've been, and are, the best of daughters. That's one of the reasons why you'd make a good wife.'

She shook her head. It didn't follow at all.

'What's he up to?' shouted Mrs Hargreaves.

Eva mouthed, 'Don't worry, mother,' and said to Lloyd, 'We'll have some tea.'

She thought: it could be all right. Lloyd had always been all right to her. He was undemanding – that is, he had been undemanding. Of course men have urges. They could be possessed. She stood, in the kitchen, transfixed at the memory of the man approaching – for twenty-five years now she had had the memory – of the man bent forward, strong, open mouth, shining eyes, half drunk – even at that time, arms wide with those huge hands coming to grasp, to encircle, smother, to crush so powerfully she feared he would break her. She closed her eyes. All on a quiet, warm, early summer evening in the park as she had strolled happily along. She had been thirteen.

All right, all right, but men weren't all the same. Lloyd – what was the matter with him tonight? – he wasn't, wasn't . . . a passionate man. He wasn't that way at all.

What she would really like, she thought, would be to manage a further, a second, afternoon class. She was in a cookery one now. The second would have to be something useful, like cookery, otherwise her mother would never agree to her going out. Oh, there were all kinds.

During tea Eva twice moved her foot away when Lloyd tried to touch it with his. She was talking all the time about cookery. Suddenly his hand came down on hers and held it tight. She flushed and trembled.

Lloyd said: 'I've something to say, Eva. If I don't say it, I'll despise myself.'

'What's he doing to you, Eva?' her mother shouted, and Lloyd shouted back, 'I'll tell you in a moment, Mrs Hargreaves.'

'Eva,' he began again, then interrupted himself. 'You know I wish we could get together some evening. I never see you without your mother.'

'She was with me when I was in trouble, all the time,' said Eva. 'I'm not deserting her,' and she withdrew her hand.

'She's going to be a problem,' he said.

'She's my problem, Lloyd.'

He sighed and leaned back in his chair. 'Eva,' he spoke carefully. 'I think it is important, very important, to each of us, that we marry. We're not young any more. And we get on well with each other. But I'm not just proposing to you because I think it's sensible. I want to marry you, Eva.'

'Eva,' shouted Mrs Hargreaves, 'what's he looking at you like that for? What's he saying? Eva, look at me, will you?'

'Please, mother, control yourself.'

'Is he . . . is he . . . going to take you away from me? He doesn't want to marry you, does he? Does he? What will happen to me then, Eva?'

'Mother, please.'

'He doesn't think of that. I'm just your mother. It would be the end of me. And you mustn't care for me, or you wouldn't just sit there.'

'Really, mother, all I do for you. I do little else but look after you.'

'Deep down, Eva, you only care for yourself. I've always known that. You're aery faery, really. Aery faery.'

Mrs Hargreaves struggled to get up from the table although by two or three delicacies she had not reached the end of her meal. Eva helped her back into the easy chair.

'She's not aery faery when she lifts you about,' Lloyd said. 'She must be as strong as a crane.'

'Oh, if only I could understand.' Tears came into Mrs Hargreaves eyes and slowly ran down her face.

'Mother,' Eva knelt down in front of her and shuffling forward held her mother's face between her hands. Their faces were only a few inches apart, with Eva's slightly lower. Eva spoke slowly and distinctly.

'I will not leave you. I will look after you. You will be all right. Understand?'

Mrs Hargreaves, eyes wide, quietened, nodded, as if in awe.

Lloyd was staring at Eva. 'Do you often do that?' he said.

'When I have to get through to her. Perhaps once a day; it depends.'

'On your knees like that,' he said. 'And do you know what you said? A bit extreme, wasn't it?'

She shook her head. Why was he questioning her? She didn't like him when he was pushing his face forward: his eyes, his mouth, his nose, his chin all seemed to be harder.

'We want a life too, you and me, Eva. Don't we? Look at me. Look at me, Eva. Thing'll have to be shared a bit, you know. It's not as if you're the only one in the family.'

She was silent.

'I didn't like to see you grovelling on the floor, on your knees, like that,' he said.

'I wasn't grovelling,' she said lightly, taking things into the kitchen.

When she came back Lloyd said, 'Sorry I used the word grovelling, Eva. Of course, you weren't. I haven't been down on my knees since I used to go to church.'

'That's your loss, Lloyd. It's just the only way I can be really sure that she understands. Are we going to play cards and stop talking?'

She chatted brightly when they played. Then he said, 'If I could have come with permission for you to attend a crochet class rather than with a proposal of marriage you'd have jumped up and kissed me, wouldn't you? . . . I can't play,' he let his cards fall. 'I don't understand you. I've asked you to marry me. You haven't said anything.'

How could she explain to him, without making him go away and never come back? How could she tell him of that dread, that fear of groping hands, searching mouth, great breathing, the grip and power of limbs, the force of the body. . . . She could not talk of any of that. If he would just let his words sink in, let them lie with her, and see what happened. Although nothing could happen. But . . . but . . . she might suddenly change; feel different. Now, it could only be, if he would promise not to go to bed with her . . . not even to touch her.

'I thought you'd be excited, thrilled,' he said.

She said, 'It's . . . it's such a great change . . . too great.'

'Look,' Lloyd said, 'I'm not asking you to marry me tomorrow. I'm no asking you to desert your mother. We'll probably all have to live together. I hope I can keep my temper because she's a selfish old woman.'

'I know that.'

She glanced at her mother who was watching with bulging eyes.

'Please, Lloyd,' she said, 'can we leave it over?'

'Till when?'

She would have liked to have said, for two or three years. 'You're pressing me,' she complained. 'I don't want any change for the moment, thank you.'

'You don't know what you're saying,' he said. Then he got up and stood by her. 'Get up,' he commanded, 'and sit down in that armchair over there.'

When she was seated in the armchair Lloyd knelt before her, took her face between his hands and ignoring Mrs Hargreaves, said: 'You are turning down my proposal of marriage. I could be the last chance you'll get to marry. I love you and I'll be with you in these years with

54

your mother, and after them. There'll be companionship, God willing, for years as well as love. And you'll have more money. There'll be my money coming in. I'm not badly paid. You'll probably live better than ever before. So, I'm offering love, companionship, and easier and richer living. Right,' he smiled and took his hands away. 'Well?'

'Marry someone else,' she said.

He stood up. 'My, God.'

She made an attempt at explanation. 'I couldn't . . . I couldn't . . . you know, that side of it . . . I'm not . . . I'm not for marrying.'

'You think I wouldn't be gentle?'

She turned her head away. 'I'm sure you would.'

'That would not be enough, being gentle, considerate?'

'No, I'm afraid not,' she muttered. He was silent and she kept her head averted just waiting for him to go.

'You'll never know what a big thing that was for me to offer to take on your mother,' he said.

'I know,' she said, 'but I would have done everything.'

'I'll not be seeing you again,' Lloyd said. 'I couldn't.' He was not all that far from sobbing. 'I'll see myself out.' She listened to the living room door opening and closing, his hurried steps along the passage and the slamming of the outer door.

'Temper,' shouted Mrs Hargreaves. 'Thank heavens, the man's gone. I've been shouting here. He wanted to marry you, didn't he?'

'Yes.'

'That would mean sleeping with him. You know that, don't you? He'd expect that. . . . He'll leave us alone in peace, Eva. Men think they can come in and just take over. Oh, I'm glad he's gone.'

Eva looked at her mother: at the thick trembling lips, the pale flabby face and chins, the small eyes gleaming now in satisfaction. The shaking of the hands was now a hand-dance of celebration. Eva felt her lips curl in revulsion, yet she knew it would not make one iota of difference in her care of her mother.

It was not good that she was now dependant on her mother for company. She knew, though, what she would do. There was a pleasant, friendly woman in the cookery class, who seemed to be lonely. She would invite her in, make a friend of her. Yet even as she pictured the possible new friend in the house a dismaying lump of fear rose within her. Fear of what she would think of her rejection of Lloyd in time ahead.

'I'll make you a cup of coffee,' she said, but she didn't hear her mother's reply. Tears flowed down her face. 'You're crying,' Mrs Hargreaves announced.

Eva dabbed her face. 'I'll make the coffee.'

'When I'm gone,' Mrs Hargreaves said, 'you might think dif You'll have no one to talk to, see. People change. He migh† still be about – that Lloyd – if you want him. If you can take his pawing. it'll not matter to me then. It's how you feel.'

Eva could still hear the slamming of the door – sense its finality. Or . . . or . . . did it only sound as if it was the end?

Mr Johnson &
Mrs Salisbury

That there were more women about than men didn't matter much to Charlie Johnson. Anyway, many of them didn't know where they were, and moaned on about going home. Some wanted their mothers. They were nearly all too fat, ate too much, and did nothing but sit about and watch the blasted television. The television had driven him out of the two main lounges.

The men were a little better, although they had to be watched as they could become nasty, unless, that is, like some of the women, they were sunk in despair. Most of the men read, argued, one or two still backed horses and there was always some football talk.

He found a peaceful place in a light armchair near the lift off the main corridor, sitting there on his own smoking his pipe and reading. The lift worked quietly and he didn't mind the little breaks it brought with its occasional traffic of people shuffling out and in, sometimes alone, sometimes assisted.

He had let the staff know what he thought about the unliveable-with television sets. All his life Charlie Johnson had been a bad man to get on the wrong side of. To be treated fairly, with no bias against him, that was all he asked. He didn't look for any preference. As long as people were reasonable and civilised, Charlie, eighty-nine years old and a widower for twenty years, was no trouble.

Then Venetia arrived. She was ninety-two and had been a widow for nearly forty years. She could neither see nor hear well, but she was thin, fairly tall and she held herself proudly, like a queen. And she had a pleasing face. Charlie thought the lines on it gave her dignity and interest. She found the television which she confused with people trying to talk to her, was so wearing that she too sought for peacefulness elsewhere and came to the corridor beside the lift.

'You're sitting in my chair,' Charlie said.

'Yes, it is a nice chair,' said Venetia. 'Thank you, My name is Mrs

Salisbury. The people here, the staff, call me by my christian name, Venetia, but they should call me Mrs Salisbury until we are familiar. Don't you agree, Mr . . . er, Mr . . .'

'Johnson. Charles Johnson. And I agree very much.' Charlie hit the wood arm of the chair so hard that Mrs Salisbury was confused. 'They patronise – that's the word – because they haven't time to be respectful, and they're so young – fifty, sixty years younger. To them we're past it, not really part of proper life. That's why they called me Charlie straightaway, the first minute I came in – they didn't know me.'

'I shall call you Mr . . . Mr . . . what was it?'

'Johnson, Mrs Salisbury.'

'Mr Johnson.'

'I'll get a chair for myself, if you don't mind,' said Charlie, 'I like sitting here.'

'Of course not, Mr Johnson'.

She told him later: 'It was her doing. But I shouldn't speak against her really, after all, she's not my flesh and blood. Mind, there were things, Stuart, my son, couldn't help me with, you know, so she, had to sort of help. She didn't like it, I could tell. But I shouldn't have given up my own house before that. I could go out of here and still manage.'

Charlie made loyal noises.

Mrs Salisbury added: 'I told them I'd walk out of here one night and go down to the river and drown myself.'

Charlie hadn't thought of the river for a long time, even though his family rarely visited him. Not like Stuart Salisbury and his wife, both about seventy themselves. They visited Mrs Salisbury at least every other day, talking to her for all of the hour or so they were there, combing her hair, getting exta shawls if she needed or wanted them, checking her room, offering her sweets and biscuits, and holding her hand. Charlie thought that was the ultimate – to hold Venetia's hand by the hour.

They were nice to him too. Chatting to him about football, going into the library room for a new book for him, even going outside to get a newspaper he fancied. Nice people. A nice family, he thought. Civilised.

It was the best time for Charlie since he came to the home. One day he heard cheerful Doreen on the staff call: 'I'll take the tea down to Venetia and Charlie.' His eyes filled with tears. He was so happy and proud.

Then Bob Saunders became resident. Charlie had known him from workdays – they were the same age – and didn't like him. He was a round-shouldered, red and rat-faced little man who shuffled about in slippers and was bent forward over his frame. After a few days he asked for a chair to be placed on the other side of Venetia and he sat there.

'You're not wanted here,' Charlie said. 'Get back to where you came from. We don't want you sitting here, understand.'

'Speak for yourself', said Bob.

'I'm speaking for the two of us.'

'She hasn't said anything.'

Venetia said, 'What's it all about – this shouting?'

Indignation having effect Charlie patted her hand and called her by her christian name. 'Never mind, Venetia,' he said, 'I'll get him away.'

'You and who else.' said Bob.

'I'll do you, if you don't move,' said Charlie.

But Bob huddled back in his chair, pressed his lips together and stared ahead. Charlie knew Bob could be stubborn, single-minded, and he was worried.

Suddenly Bob leant forward and put a hand over Venetia's and said: 'My name's Bob. I think you're a fine looking woman. I've had a look at them all here. They're not much to crack about. You're streets ahead. You're like my wife was. She was good looking.'

Venetia said, 'Thank you. My name's Mrs Salisbury. Venetia Salisbury.'

'Don't tell him your christian name,' barked Charlie.

'Everybody knows it, stupid,' said Bob.

'Stupid!' said Charlie, 'and how dare you talk to her . . .' and then he saw Bob's hand over Venetia's. 'Take that away,' he yelled. 'Get it off.'

'Please, please,' remonstrated Venetia. 'Noise.'

Charlie grabbed hold of Bob's hand and tried to wrench it away. Bob tightened his hold. Venetia struggled to extricate her hand and eventually succeeded. 'Really,' she exclaimed.

Bob then patted her knee, 'Never mind, pet,' he said. 'He can't keep his temper, Charlie. Never could.'

Charlie was struggling to get on his feet.

'You'll have a fit and die,' said Bob.

'Don't do that . . . Charlie,' said Venetia.

'It makes no difference if you live or die,' said Bob, ''Cos she's mine.'

'She's not,' gasped Charlie.

'She is, because I love her,' said Bob.

Charlie now on his feet and trying to work out how he could hit Bob with his stick which he needed to keep on his feet, was nonplussed and stared at Bob, who said, 'And I'm going to tell her that again, when we're on our own, that I love her. You never told her that, did you? Because you daren't. You haven't the courage. And you don't, see.'

'Do you, Charlie?' said Venetia.

'I do,' said Charlie quickly, than added, 'I think so.'

'I said it first, anyway,' said Bob. 'Venetia's mine.'

'Venetia's nobody's,' said Venetia, 'And it's Mrs Salisbury to you. "Venetia's mine"' she repeated scornfully. ' Charlie, when he stands up, if he can manage it, when the gong goes, swipe his frame away from him with your stick. He'll fall and break something, a leg or an arm or his neck. And they'll take him to the hospital and keep him in. He might never come back – he might die there.'

Charlie said: 'I think you are, if I may say so, Venetia, a very fine woman indeed for saying that. And if he comes out I'll swipe his frame away again.'

Yesterday's Paper

Early in 1920 my mother was handed Aunt Sadie's stillborn child wrapped up in a torn-off, worn, flannel sheet by the woman from the next street who helped in such emergencies.

Aunt Sadie gasped, 'Vi.'

'Yes, Sadie.'

'Give it to a kind man at the cemetery, will you.'

'I will, love.'

Looking at the wrapped up dead child mother thought that everyone would guess what it was so she picked up the top newspaper – the previous day's North Mail – from those under a cushion and wrapped that round too.

The helping woman followed her into the passage. 'Carry it in a shopping bag, pet' she whispered. 'Be easier. There's one in the kitchen. I'll get it.'

But when mother felt the little weight at the bottom of the bag she crinkled her face and said, 'It doesn't seem right, somehow. I'd rather carry it in my arms.'

So she set out for the cemetery. She'd been told where it was and that she couldn't miss it. Mother knew she could miss it but that she would find it eventually. If matters became desperate someone would take pity on her and escort her, and then she would confide in her or him what was in the wrapped up newspaper.

Feeling important she asked her way frequently so in fact she went the wrong way only once and pretty soon she was told she was all right as she was in Cemetery Road. Mother, who had very little schooling, hadn't known, as she couldn't make head or tail of street names.

She went straight to the lodge and asked the kind looking and voiced man who came to the door if he would have the stillborn child put in a nice person's grave, and the man said that that was no trouble, canny woman, and that he would see to it himself.

When she returned pleased and proud, the woman helper was ready to go and Aunt Sadie sitting on a hard chair and resting her head against the brass bedrails said, 'There's a ten shilling note in my purse, Vi, in the top drawer there. Will you give it to Mrs Wallace.'

Mrs Wallace was impressed and murmured that seeing it had been stillborn, seven and six would do, but Aunt Sadie shook her head, her eyes closed.

When they were on their own mother said, 'That was a lot of money, Sadie. You could have got away with five shillings, never mind the seven and six she talked about.'

Aunt Sadie shook her head, so mother did some quick and expert clearing up and tidying up and began to prepare a meal for Uncle Ted.

Aunt Sadie and Uncle Ted had had to get married before the war, in 1913: mother hadn't, so this gave her a lifelong feeling of moral superiority over Aunt Sadie, but much of the enjoyment of this was lost because Aunt Sadie's first child had come three weeks before her own first child, and she and Dad had been married since 1911.

Uncle Ted had been a tall, slim, callow young man working in a barber's shop. Aunt Sadie was more intelligent, harder-working and sharper-tongued, and she was intent on making a success of the marriage. The war made this difficult as when Uncle Ted came back from it he was a man who could stick up for himself loudly at times, and who knew that there were a fair number of young women around who liked the look of him.

He liked my mother, but had to be careful as my father, his eldest brother, had a stronger personality and could be dangerously jealous. When Uncle Ted came in that day the sight of his pale, exhausted and distressed wife killed off any inclination to banter with my mother. Not because of overwhelming sympathy with Aunt Sadie, but because he sensed that it wasn't an appropriate time. He gazed with distaste at Aunt Sadie.

Aunt Sadie glanced at him and said, 'Stillborn. Vi took it to the cemetery. It was a boy.'

After a while Uncle Ted said, 'A boy. Dead, like.'

'Yes,' said mother, 'It never lived, poor thing. . . . The man said he'd see it was placed in a nice person's grave.'

'Hmf. How would he know if the person was nice,' said Uncle Ted. 'He'd have no more idea than the man in the moon.'

Mother's chin came up: 'He'd know,' she said. 'They hear things. It will be in someone's arms.'

Aunt Sadie began to sob.

Mother said to Uncle Ted, 'Sadie had to pay Mrs Wallace.'

'Vi,' Aunt Sadie remonstrated wearily, shaking her head.

'Mrs Wallace? Whose she? Pay her for what?'

'For helping.'

Uncle Ted had to absorb this.

'Vi, men don't understand these things. You should know that.' Aunt Sadie said.

'How much . . . what sort of money are we talking about, like?' he asked Aunt Sadie.

Aunt Sadie managed to shrug her shoulders, 'Nothing,' she said.

'Ten bob,' said mother. 'Ten bob,' nodding her head at him as if it were all his fault.

'Hell,' exclaimed Uncle Ted.

'Don't swear, Ted,' Aunt Sadie said, 'And Vi, why did you tell him? It has nothing to do with Ted. He need never have known.'

'It's money out of the house,' said Uncle Ted gravely. 'Money I've had to work for.'

Aunt Sadie said, 'It was money well spent. I'm alive.'

'That's very true,' said mother. Uncle Ted was speechless. After a minute or so Aunt Sadie turned her head away and began to cry. Later she dried her eyes, and said, 'Give Ted his tea, Vi, will you.'

When he was having his corned beef Uncle Ted said to Aunt Sadie, 'You're not havin' any, then?'

'Couldn't.'

'There's something in yesterday's North Mail I want to see,' he said. 'Where is it?'

'It'll be under the cushion if it's not about,' said Aunt Sadie.

'Well, it's not about, is it,' he said, 'that's today's.' He got up and pulled out the newspapers from under the cushion and he went through them. 'It's not here,' he announced. He looked through them again. 'It's not among them.'

Mother said quietly, 'Then, it'll be up at the cemetery. I got the newspaper to wrap it in from under that cushion.'

'Ye didn't,' exclaimed Uncle Ted. 'You took the top one, Vi, didn't ye. Why couldn't ye take one of the others. Look at all of them.'

'It couldn't have served a better purpose,' Aunt Sadie said. 'I wish I felt better.'

Mother snapped. 'As if I had time to see which day's paper it was.'

Both Uncle Ted and Aunt Sadie doubted if she'd have known which day's paper it was even if she'd scanned them, but they didn't say anything about that.

Uncle Ted said, 'Damn. Sick'nin'. I wanted to see something very much in that paper. About a chap who comes into the shop. Really.'

'You goin' on about yesterday's paper,' said mother. 'get another. And there's something of you too in that paper, now. Not that you'll ever understand.'